TEA PARTY:
AMERICAN REVOLUTION 2.0

Silent Majority Silent No More

By

Robin Rohr

Library of Congress July 29, 2010
ISBN-1453698558

Dedication

To American Patriots,
Past, Present, and Future,
Who believe in One Nation Under God,
Indivisible with Liberty and Justice for All.

Acknowledgments

With heartfelt appreciation I would like to acknowledge my husband, **Mike Carter**, for his unwavering support of this project, and for his uncanny ability to track down quotes and transcripts, for being my IT department and keeping me linked to the Internet, for designing the cover, and for his technical expertise in transferring this manuscript into compatible formats for electronic publication. My deepest thanks go to my neighbors and friends, **Cindy and Rod Panzer,** for their invaluable comments and suggestions regarding the manuscript, with special kudos to **Cindy** for the tenacity she displayed while editing. And, to **Sue Ellin Browder**, my friend and mentor, who said those fateful words, "You ought to write a book". Thank you all for your belief, support, and prayers during the writing of this chronicle.

3

Table of Contents

The Gadsden Flag
"Don't Tread on Me"

The historic "Don't Tread on Me" banner is prominent at modern Tea Party rallies, and by popular usage it has become the unofficial "official" flag for the movement.

The yellow banner was designed and named after Continental Colonel and statesman Christopher Gadsden in 1775. Gadsden served on the original Continental Congress Committee that was charged with outfitting the first naval mission, including the original contingent of what would become the United States Marines. Those first Marines adopted the Gadsden banner as their personal motto and flag.

Before the departure of that first mission, Gadsden presented the banner to the newly appointed Commander-in-Chief of the Navy, Commodore Esek Hopkins, and a copy of the flag to the legislature in his home state of South Carolina.

In December 1775, Benjamin Franklin, writing under the pseudonym "American Guesser", described the rattlesnake as a perfect symbol for the American spirit:

> *"I recollected that her eye excelled in brightness, that of any other animal, and that she has no eye-lids, she may therefore be esteemed an emblem of vigilance.*
>
> *She never begins an attack, nor, when once engaged, ever surrenders: She is therefore an emblem of magnanimity and true courage.*
>
> *As if anxious to prevent all pretensions of quarreling with her, the weapons with which nature has*

furnished her, she conceals in the roof of her mouth, so that, to those who are unacquainted with her, she appears to be a most defenseless animal; and even when those weapons are shewn and extended for her defense, they appear weak and contemptible; but their wounds however small, are decisive and fatal: Conscious of this, she never wounds till she has generously given notice, even to her enemy, and cautioned him against the danger of treading on her.

Was I wrong, Sir, in thinking this a strong picture of the temper and conduct of America?"

Introduction

Tea Parties are the public expression of a great patriotic awakening within the American people. Today, tens of millions of citizens are committing themselves to restoring the principles and values of our founding fathers, and to re-establishing fidelity to the United States Constitution as the working framework for our government. After their opinions were ignored by elected officials and the establishment media alike, everyday folks began to express their own messages utilizing the most basic form of political speech: a homemade sign.

Throughout the history of human civilization the norm has been one of the common man suffering under the tyranny of elites. The shining exception has been the United States of America, which was uniquely established by the people for the people. At the time of the first Revolution the population was split in its thinking: one-third supported the patriots, one-third was loyal to the crown, and one-third wanted to be left alone. It was just one-third of the population that overthrew the tyranny of the aristocracy. The same is true today, except that more of the "want to be left alones" are joining with the patriots.

Our founding fathers bequeathed to us a governing document based upon the liberty of the individual, with checks and balances designed to ensure that liberty. Those checks have been eroded over the last one hundred years, resulting in the balance of power being tipped away from the people and towards an elite ruling class who deem themselves far superior to, and wiser than, "ordinary" citizens.

With the awakening of the silent majority, it is those ordinary citizens who are now answering the call from patriots past and present to rescue our Constitution. They are hardworking people who are taking a closer look at the corruption and unaccountability in Washington, and they fear for the future of their children and their country.

The vast silent majority are educating themselves, talking with family and friends, and meeting up with other same-minded citizens to demand that political power be restored to the people. They are willing to publicly demonstrate against the blatant threats to their liberty being perpetrated against them by their own government. In seven short months the Tea Party Movement grew from local events attended by a few hundred people, to a massive national rally of over one million citizens before the Capitol Building in Washington D.C.

The unprecedented growth of this American grassroots movement could not have been achieved without the widespread ownership of personal computers and the aid of the Internet. The "2.0" in the title, **TEA PARTY: AMERICAN REVOLUTION 2.0**, is a reference to the power of the computer in the hands of everyday Americans. The same power given to the Revolutionary pamphleteers through the printing press is now used by modern patriots, via a computer, to exercise their rights of free speech. When a software program is updated the new version is designated by the number of the revision, 2.0, 3.0, etc. Just so, the Tea Party Movement is dedicated to the renewal of the values of our founders, and the restoration of the U.S. Constitution as the governing document of our land. This movement is the modern equivalent of the original fight for the right of the individual to be free from the oppression of a small governing elite. It is the American Revolution 2.0.

As with the Sons of Liberty who dumped tea into Boston Harbor, the concerns of modern-day Tea Party participants run much deeper than mere dissatisfaction with taxes. The movement is the public manifestation of the profound love the modern patriot feels for his country. It is the deep and abiding love that inspires a patriot to defend his country when its liberty is threatened. The same brave love for freedom that inspired the first American revolutionaries to fight the tyranny of the crown, and to establish a government based upon rights endowed by our Creator. These are the God-given rights of life, liberty, property, and the pursuit of happiness for every individual without fear of retribution from another, or from the government. It is the desire to restore these rights and freedoms won for us over two centuries ago, which is giving voice to the silent majority.

This same love of liberty and freedom has fueled other historical hinges in the American experience as well, when the soul of the nation was cleansed, strengthened, and renewed. The great religious revival of the 1840's energized the liberty-loving abolitionist movement, and the freedom-loving pioneers questing west forged a nation out of the continent they conquered. The modern Tea Party Movement is just such a hinge in history and will be studied by historians for decades to come. If successful, it will remake the political landscape of America.

11

Tea Party people are dedicated to the restoration of liberty and the preservation of the free society secured by their fathers, grandfathers and great-grandfathers. Theirs is a battle of gallant proportions, and the foot soldiers in this battle are deeply committed to their cause, as to a higher calling. This honorable love and commitment compels the patriots to willingly sacrifice their time, energy and money to ensure that the rights of the free individual will always be upheld and protected in America. This noble political odyssey deserves to be described boldly and passionately.

Yet, Tea Party people are denigrated and derided by the establishment press. Academic elites dismiss them as ignorant and backward. The career politicians deride them as an "angry mob". The citizens participating in the Tea Parties are insulted and offended by the press coverage and by the attitudes of their elected representatives. They ache to see their story told by an understanding witness. This is their story.

The story of the American Revolution 2.0.

Chapter One

The Spark:
Spot Fires of Freedom

*"As parents, we can have no joy, knowing that
this government is not sufficiently lasting
to ensure any thing which we may bequeath to posterity:
And by a plain method of argument,
as we are running the next generation into debt,
we ought to do the work of it,
otherwise we use them meanly and pitifully."*
- Thomas Paine, "Common Sense", 1776

A modern citizen's revolt has been brewing in America among the silent majority for many years, and the kettle began to boil in late 2008 and into the beginning months of 2009 as the country slipped into a deep economic recession. The tone-deaf congress passed tax and spending bills reaching into the stratosphere, and adding insult to injury, that august body arrogantly passed these massive bills without even reading their contents. Out-of-control spending by the Republican-led congress had resulted in their loss of the majority in the House and Senate in the 2006 elections.[1] However, in spite of their 2006 and 2008 election rhetoric, the Democrat controlled congress was hell-bent on quadrupling the national budget deficit in record time.

---

[1] The Republican Party gained the majority in the House of Representatives in the 1994 election with a unified platform known as "Contract for America'.

13

In early October 2008 congress passed TARP (Troubled Asset Relief Program) costing $800 billion. TARP allowed the Treasury Secretary to purchase non-liquid, difficult-to-value assets from banks and other financial institutions. Republican President George W. Bush and Treasury Secretary Henry Paulson presented the bill to congress as an emergency response to possible massive bank failures in multiple institutions.

Senator Dianne Feinstein (D-CA) stated from the floor of the Senate, "You know they say senators have six year terms so that they can take tough votes when tough votes are called for. So that they can vote for the best interest of their country, even sometimes, when their constituents don't understand it or may be opposed to it." She continued, "I've received 91,000 phone calls and emails from California, 85,000 of them opposed to this measure. There is a great deal of confusion out there. People don't understand."[2] With a 93% opposition from her constituents, this comment raises the question: If the people don't understand the contemplated actions of congress, shouldn't the senators take the time, and make the effort, to explain to the people the proposed legislation before voting for passage?

The Democrat majority in both houses passed the proposal, quickly and with little debate, over the strenuous protestation of taxpayers. Fiscal-conservative Republicans were shut out of the debate, and were only able to mount a modest opposition. TARP funding was quickly used beyond its scope to

---

[2] Senator Diane Feinstein, October 1, 2008. Reported on Campaign for Liberty website: http:///www.campaignforliberty.com/user/kenmack/

bail out auto manufacturers General Motors (GM) and Chrysler, and the insurance giant American International Group, Inc. (AIG).

In February of 2009, the Stimulus Bill was presented with the same supposed urgency. The American Recovery and Reinvestment Act 2009 will cost the taxpayer $787 billion, including interest the total is over one trillion dollars. With limited committee action before voting, it was passed over the citizenry's vigorous objections, by all but eleven Democrats (a number insufficient to impact the majority voting block). In an uncharacteristic, but welcomed, show of solidarity all Republicans voted against the bill. President Barack Obama signed the bill into law on February 17, 2009. Elected officials, in just a few short months, had put the taxpayer, their children and grandchildren on the hook for 1.7 trillion dollars.

Americans, raised to respect their elected officials and the everyday workings of a representative Republic, tried to communicate with their elected office-holders through letter writing, telephone calls, faxes, and email. However, congressional actions made it ever more apparent that these forms of communication were useless. Citizens received form letter responses that resembled public relations pushes more than an honest communication with a constituent. The lament for years by those concerned had become, "What else can I do?"

Americans are by nature an independent people. When push comes to shove, more often than not, they shove back. Spot fires of freedom began to flare.

By the second week in February, Keli Carender of Seattle WA, who blogs[3] under the name "Liberty Belle", began to spread the word about a grassroots protest she was organizing to express opposition to the Stimulus Bill. Opponents began to call it the "Porkulus Bill" because 90% of the spending was earmarked for projects in favored congressional districts, and grants to protect state and local government jobs.

With no experience in political organizing, with no connections to corporate lobbyists or a think tank organization, this conservative mom reached out on the Internet, called her local talk radio station, and talked to anyone who would listen. One of those who listened was Michelle Malkin, syndicated columnist, hostess of a popular website, and best-selling author. Malkin jokingly pledged to support the rally by bringing a roast pig for lunch. Indeed, Malkin did much more than that. It appears she unintentionally acted as mid-wife to the birth of a new era of watchful citizenship. In just a few days Carender planned and organized the ad hoc event.[4]

On Monday February 16th an energetic crowd of about 100 people came together in downtown Seattle. Those present were from all walks of life, of all ages from children to seniors, middle-aged men and women, and young families. Michelle Malkin served up the promised roast pig. Waving American flags, and sporting several "Don't Tread On Me" banners, this group of average working Americans came with home-made signs

---

[3] "Blog" is a contraction of the term 'web log' where individuals write about topics of interest to themselves and others on websites.
[4] As reported on the Michelle Malkin website April 15, 2009 "A Tax Day Tea Party Cheat Sheet, How It All Started": http://michellemalkin.com/2009/04/15/a-tax-day-tea-party-cheat-sheet-how-it-all-started/

that emphasized the depth of their opposition to the recent actions of congress, such as "Stimulate Business Not Government".

A little girl held a piece of brown cardboard proclaiming, "I don't want to pay for the Swindle Us Package!" and underneath in parenthesis, "I'm only 10 years old!" Another girl, curled up in a camp chair, held a sign "Families Against Porkulus". A young man, wearing a Cat-in-the-Hat style American flag hat and a rubber pig nose held a sign saying, "Say NO to Generational Theft". One sign proclaimed, "Atlas Will Shrug", which is a reference to Ayn Rand's 1958 novel "*Atlas Shrugged*". (In the novel, industrialists, inventors, artists, and other productive people respond to burdensome and punitive regulations by refusing to provide any more for the "looters and moochers". By their economic inactivity they break the government stranglehold on society and restore individualism and free markets.)

News about the Seattle protest began to spread across the Internet through Michelle Malkin's site and other bloggers. Website posters[5] pointed out that there should be a protest in Denver on February 17th to greet President Obama when he came to that city to sign the Stimulus Bill at a staged event. The Denver Chapter of Americans for Prosperity (AFP) had already begun putting something together, and with little traditional advertising, hundreds attended the rally at the Colorado State Capitol.

Michelle Malkin reported on her website, "I met the head of the [Colorado] state AFP for the first time on the steps of the Capitol. [It was a] union of like minds in an impromptu show of

---

[5] "Posters" refers to blog readers who submit commentary to, or directly comment on the content of, a blog or website.

outrage against the legislation-without-deliberation process in Washington."

The rally attracted people from a wide spectrum of the political landscape. Also present at the Denver event was Jon Caldara from the libertarian think tank Independence Institute, as well as former congressional representative Tom Tancredo, advocating the strict enforcement of current immigration laws. Many attending were angry about the deliberate exclusion of E-Verify standards from Stimulus funded projects. E-Verify is a government program that allows employers, via the Internet, to check the legal residency status of potential employees.

On February 18th approximately 500 taxpayers rallied in Mesa AZ to oppose President Obama's plans to expand the federal government home mortgage entitlement program. The program would allow holders of sub-prime mortgages to modify agreements by lowering interest rates, restructuring pay back schedules and make other financial arrangements to help homeowners remain in their houses, all backed by the federal treasury. If homeowners still defaulted on their loans, taxpayers would be ultimately responsible for the loss. The event in Mesa was organized and promoted by the local talk radio station, KFYI. There was no national organization involved. There was no national media coverage.

That same week, Amanda Grosserode of Overland Park KS, was also "fed up" with the spending in Washington. "I didn't know about anything else happening on the national level. Then someone told me about Michelle Malkin's website."[6]

---

[6] Amanda Grosserode: Telephone interview November 6, 2009.

18

On February 19th Grosserode emailed Malkin that she was organizing a tax revolt protest in Overland Park, Kansas, for the upcoming weekend. Enlisting the help of family and friends to spread the word her efforts received attention from Fair Tax Kansas City, a group she had joined the previous fall, and the local talk radio station.[7]

Bundling up against the sunny 25-degree weather, between 500 and 700 taxpayers came to protest the Stimulus Bill at Democrat Congressman Dennis Moore's office. They lined the street with American flags flying in the winter wind and their homemade signs held aloft proclaiming, "No More Moore", "No Moore Pork" and "Freedom of Speech for Conservatives Too!" Reports from participants included the observation of the driver of a U.S. Mail truck honking and waving in support.

Once again there was no major media reporting of the event. Glenn Reynolds, a pioneer of the blogosphere,[8] began to post details on his widely read website "Instapundit". A poster who attended the event stated, "It was cold and windy, but not bitter…we were warmed by all the support we got from passing traffic. I'd call it a huge success!"[9]

The citizens who showed up at the impromptu tax revolts shared an outrage at the lack of fiscal responsibility by both political parties, and frustration with the apparent inability of their elected officials to take their constituents concerns seriously.

---

[7] As reported on Michelle Malkin April 15, 2009 "A Tax Day Tea Party Cheat Sheet-How It All Started": http://michellemalkin.com/2009/04/15/a-tax-day-tea-party-cheat-sheet-how-it-all-started/

[8] "Blogosphere" refers to the realm of the Internet inhabited by blogs; a universal term for all blog websites.

[9] As reported on Instapundit February 22, 2009 "Overland Park Taxpayers' Protest": http://pajamasmedia.com/instapundit/?s=Tax+Day+Tea+Party

They were worried and angry over government bailouts for banks, corporations, and individuals who had made irresponsible choices; over so-called stimulus money spent on government projects and programs; and over federal borrowing to cover current spending that would enslave their children and grandchildren for decades to come.

Those attending the tax revolts also had a better grasp of basic economics than the elites in Washington. They understood you can't spend your way out of debt with money you don't have, and that borrowed money could only be repaid through higher taxes. They also feared government-caused inflation resulting from the printing of un-backed currency, which would lead to a devalued dollar, depleted buying power, and sinking savings.

On February 19, 2009 cable television financial analyst Rick Santelli[10], poured gasoline on the spot fires, and inadvertently gave the tax revolt movement its name: Tea Party. The video clip became known as "Rick's Rant", and it struck a responsive chord in citizens disgusted with the inept handling of the economy by Washington elites.

Anchors on the CNBC program "*Squawk Box*" were discussing President Obama's plan to bail out homeowners who could no longer make their payments on sub-prime mortgages. The modification plan provided $75 billion to reach an estimated 9 million homeowners over five years.

---

[10] Rick Santelli is a former trader at the Chicago Mercantile Exchange and a currency specialist.

Guest panelist Wilbur Ross[11] asked, "Does anyone really think that all that keeps nine million people from losing their homes is $1,600 per year [in mortgage payment adjustments]?" He concluded, "I don't think so."

Reporting from the traders' pit at the Chicago Mercantile Exchange, Rick Santelli was asked if he was listening to the in-studio conversation. In the minutes that followed, Santelli unconsciously voiced the thoughts shared by many of his fellow Americans who were angry because elected officials were seemingly intent on destroying the capitalist free market economic system.

"Listening to it! I've just been glued to it because Mr. Ross has nailed it! The government is promoting bad behavior because we certainly don't want to put stimulus forth and give people a whopping eight or ten dollars in the [pay]check and think that they ought to save it." (The Stimulus Bill included a so-called "tax cut" for working Americans that was in actuality only a change in the withholding formula. Taxpayers would still be taxed at the same rate, but would have less withholding available in April 2010 to meet their obligation.)

Santelli continued, "And, in terms of modifications, I'll tell you what, I have an idea: you know, the new administration is big on computers and technology, how about this, President and new administration, why don't you put up a website to have people vote on the Internet, as a referendum to see if we really want to subsidize the losers' mortgages or would we like to,

---

[11] Wilbur Ross is the Chairman and Chief Executive Officer of W.L. Ross & Co. L.L.C., a merchant banking firm.

at least, buy cars and buy houses in foreclosure, and give them to people that might actually have a chance to prosper down the road and reward people that can carry the water instead of drink the water."

A floor trader next to Santelli exclaimed, "That's a novel idea!"

"This is America!" Santelli continued, "How many of you people want to pay for your neighbor's mortgage that has an extra bathroom and can't pay their bills? Raise their hand."

Over the resounding boos that arose from the commodities traders conveying their dislike for that idea, Santelli asked, "President Obama, are you listening?"

Another trader sarcastically chimed in, "How about we all stop paying our mortgage, it's a moral hazard." An animated Santelli continued, "You know, Cuba used to have mansions and a relatively decent economy. They moved from the individual to the collective, now they're driving '54 Chevy's." As an aside, he added, "Maybe the last great car to come out of Detroit!"

Anchor Joe Kernen responded, "Wilbur pointed out, you can go down to 2% on the mortgage," with Santelli interrupting, "You could go down to minus 2%. They can't afford the house!" Kernen continued, "and still have 40% not be able to do it, so why are they in the house? Why are we trying to keep them in the house?"

Santelli replied, "I know Mr. Summers[12] is a great economist, but boy, I'd love the answer to that one!"

---

[12] Lawrence Summers is an economic advisor to the Obama Administration. He is chairman of the National Economic Council.

Anchor Rebecca Quick commented, "Wow! Wilbur, you get people fired up!" Santelli continued, "We're thinking of having a Chicago Tea Party in July. All you capitalists that want to show up to Lake Michigan, I'm going to start organizing." The traders responded with lusty cheers and whistles.

Quick asked, "What are you dumping in this time?"

Santelli responded, "I think we'll be dumping in some derivative securities, what do you think about that?" (Derivative securities bundled both sub-prime and prime mortgages into investment vehicles sold to third parties. The crash of derivatives led to the financial crisis in late 2008.)

Santelli continued, "These guys are pretty straightforward. And my guess is, a pretty good statistical cross-section of America. The silent majority."

Quick observed, "Not so silent majority. So, Rick, are they opposed to the housing thing, to the stimulus package, to everything out there?"

"You know," Santelli continued "they're pretty much of the notion that you can't buy your way into prosperity, and if the multiplier (the supposed return on the stimulus investments) that all these Washington economists are selling us is over one, then we never have to worry about the economy again. The government should spend $1 trillion an hour because we'll get $1.5 trillion back."

Wilbur Ross declared, "Rick, I congratulate you on your new incarnation as a revolutionary leader." Santelli concluded, "Somebody needs one! I'll tell you what, if you read our founding fathers, people like Benjamin Franklin and Jefferson, what we're doing in this country now is making them roll over in their graves!"

23

This segment aired at 5:11 a.m. (EST). Large portions of the audio were played later that day on the nationally syndicated *Rush Limbaugh* radio program, which begins at noon (EST). Limbaugh's show boasts a listener base of 20 million. Within twenty-four hours of the original broadcast, CNBC was flooded with over 5,000 mostly supportive emails, 1.4 million people had viewed the video of "Rick's Rant" on their website[13], and hundreds of thousands more saw it on You Tube, on other websites or in emails forwarded by friends.[14]

It was also noted in the halls of power. At a White House briefing the next day, CBS News' Chip Reid asked Press Secretary Robert Gibbs about Santelli's comments. Mr. Gibbs responded, "I also think that it's tremendously important for people who rant on cable television to be responsible and understand what it is they're talking about. I feel assured that Mr. Santelli doesn't know what he's talking about." (Rick Santelli holds a Bachelor of Science degree from the University of Illinois Champaign/Urbana. He began his career in 1979 as a trader at the Chicago Mercantile Exchange in gold, lumber, livestock, CD's, T-bills and foreign currencies. He joined CNBC as a financial analyst in 1999 after leaving Institutional Financial Futures and Options at Sanwa Futures, L.L.C.) Gibbs snidely joked that he would like to invite Santelli to the White House for some decaf coffee.[15]

---

[13] CNBC News website February 20, 2009: http://www.cnbc.com//id/29302299
[14] As of August 13, 2009 the "Rant of the Year" on You Tube had 1,078,235 viewers: http://www.youtube.com/watch?v=bEZB4taSEoA
[15] CBS News website February 20, 2009:
http://www.cbsnews.com/blogs/2009/02/20/politics/politicalhotsheet/entry481637
2.shtml?tag

Santelli, through his impassioned cry, "We're thinking of having a Chicago Tea Party", inadvertently christened the new tax revolt movement. The 1773 Boston Tea Party is buried deep in the American psyche, and all patriots know the story of the daring Sons of Liberty, donning the dress of native Indians and tossing more than 300 cases of English tea into Boston Harbor. The British response was to increase the burdensome measures imposed upon the colonies. Their actions only inflamed the independent spirit of the colonists, uniting them in common cause and leading to the American Revolution.

Americans watching television and listening to radios from coast to coast looked at their families and said, "Yeah, let's have a Tea Party!"

Contrary to later charges by the Progressive elements in the media that the tax revolt and burgeoning Tea Party movement was an invention by "right-wing" groups, the revival of watchful citizenship within the political landscape came before the assistance afforded by established conservative and libertarian organizations. These groups were just the first political organizations to recognize the universality of the concerns expressed. They understood the fire-in-the-belly that was motivating the first rallies. They recognized the power displayed as citizens, compelled by their love of liberty, went out into the street trying to get their government to listen to them. No amount of organizing or direction from established groups would have been successful without the sentiment of disgust that was palpable among the people.

25

As Samuel Adams, American patriot and cousin to John Adams the second President of the United States, wrote, "It does not take a majority to prevail…but rather an irate, tireless minority keen on…setting brushfires of freedom in the minds of men." (There is a website called "Brush Fires of Freedom", taking their name from this quote.)

Within days of the first rallies, people began to network contacts between established conservative political groups and the volunteer citizen organizers in different cities. The first group was Top Conservatives on Twitter (#TCOT)[16], founded by Michael Patrick Leahy and led by Rob Neppell. On February 21st they announced, "Simultaneous local Tea Parties around the country, beginning in Chicago, and including Washington D.C., Fayetteville NC, Omaha NE, and dozens of other locations on February 27th."

As expected in a town populated by political operatives, the locals who organized the Washington D.C. rally came from the ranks of established conservative organizations including Brendan Steinhauser from FreedomWorks, John O'Hara from the Heartland Institute, Andrew Langer of The Institute for Liberty, and J. P. Freire, a contributing editor at *The American Spectator* magazine.

Other individuals leading established groups also began to lend their expertise to the new movement. Eric Odom from the DontGo Movement (now known as the American Liberty Alliance), Jenny Beth Martin of Smart Girl Politics, Adam Waldeck from American Solutions, and Matt Kibbe at

---

[16] Twitter and Facebook are social networking sites on the Internet.

FreedomWorks, to name just a few. Organizations like Americans for Prosperity and the American Family Association soon began to disseminate information about Tea Party rallies to their memberships. Popular websites like MichelleMalkin.com and Lucianne.com chronicled the experiences of their posters on threads discussing the rallies.

In a quiet town outside Sacramento CA, Mark and Patty Meckler heard "Rick's Rant" about the Stimulus Bill and were heartened by the fact that someone on television actually said something that made sense to them. Meckler is a thirty-something lawyer working out of a small office in his home with his wife providing office support, and raising two children. Busy with their lives, becoming involved in political action was the last thing on their minds, until Meckler's mother came over for a visit.

Patty explained, "Mark's mother said to us, 'It is just awful what is happening in our country. We are the land of the free and the brave. We have to be brave to remain free.'" Without expecting much of a response, Meckler sent emails out to some friends inviting them to join forces and meet on February 27th at the State Capitol building in Sacramento. They all came back with "see you on Friday at noon." Mark turned to Patty and said, "The grassroots has spoken."

Simultaneously in San Diego, Dawn Wildman, a paralegal, was working with a group of citizens and the Heritage Foundation reviewing the Stimulus Bill trying to identify where the taxes and spending were headed, and preparing a booklet in everyday language for citizens to understand.

"The call for a modern Boston Tea Party seemed to fit right in with that," Wildman remembered. Working with her partners, Leslie Eastman and Sarah Bond, they began to email friends and contacts to join them for a Tea Party on the 27th.

At the same time, others were also busy with preparations for Tea Parties in Los Angeles CA, Houston TX, Tempe AZ, and small towns like Calera AL and Tulsa IA, all for Friday. The number of Tea Parties that day varies widely, from a dismissive ten to fifty different cities, with an estimated turnout of at least 30,000 people. All these events were organized within one week.

On that Friday morning the Mecklers checked their children out of school.

Patty Meckler reasoned, "They can learn about history in school, now they were going to see history being made. We went down to Sacramento with the kids, along with grandma and grandpa." They arrived at the State Capitol about 11:00 a.m. and Patty began to assemble the forty signs she had made for the rally. "I was on the sidewalk stapling them together," said Patty, "and telling folks to pick up whichever one appealed to them. The next thing I knew, I looked up and about 200 people were there!"

The crowd drew the attention of a Highway Patrol officer who asked the Mecklers if they had a permit for their gathering.[17] Expecting only a few friends to join them, the neophyte "organizers" had not applied for one. They accompanied the officer inside the Capitol to process the permit. Patty continued, "The crowd grew as others walking or driving by stopped and joined us. We knew we were headed into something huge."

---

[17] The California Highway Patrol provides security at the capitol.

In San Diego Dawn Wildman expected to be joined that Friday by only her family and partners. The rally was scheduled to begin at 9:00 a.m. at the Embarcadero. "We were blown away by the 500 others who showed up," Wildman remembers. "We were really taken aback at the number of people who came," she paused. "We were shocked at the turnout." After the positive response to the spending protest, Dawn Wildman, Leslie Eastman and Sarah Bond founded the Southern California Tax Revolt Coalition to continue organizing rallies in the greater San Diego county area.

That same day across the country, despite terrible weather in many regions, citizens braved the wind, rain, and cold to gather together to raise their voices against the current direction the country was heading. Over 1,500 attended at St. Louis' famous arch, in Chicago IL approximately 1,000 gathered downtown, and another estimated 1,000 at the River Place Complex in Greenville SC. Rallies were also held in smaller towns and cities such as Shelby AL, Asheville NC, and Sarasota FL.

These Americans responded to their deep concerns by exercising their rights to peaceably assemble and petition their government. The First Amendment to the U.S. Constitution guarantees "Congress shall make no law respecting … the right of the people peaceably to assemble, and to petition the government for a redress of grievances."

They flew American and "Don't Tread On Me" flags. They expressed their opinions with signs made at their kitchen tables using poster board and marker pens, or just 8x10 paper printed from their computers.

These novice sign makers often ran out of room, with the last letters of their messages trailing along the edges. Some had their signs attached to garden stakes, yardstick rulers, or just held them in their hands. Every one was a personal message, "Taxed Enough Already", "Spread My Work Ethic Not The Wealth" and "I'm Tea'd Off".

The emotions at the Tea Parties were a mixture of frustration at the breakneck speed with which these massive spending bills were being passed, and the pleasant surprise to find so many others sharing that frustration. The atmosphere at the rallies was more reminiscent of a neighborhood block party than a protest.

On March 12th, Glenn Beck, Fox News host of *"The Glenn Beck Show"* and radio personality, announced a new national initiative called the 9.12 Project.[18] He recalled to listeners and viewers the feeling in America on September 12, 2001. It was the day after the horrendous terrorist attacks in New York and Washington D.C., and citizens onboard Flight 93 gave their lives resisting the terrorists. On that day all of us were united as a country. Gone were the labels of Democrat or Republican, Progressive or Conservative. We were all Americans. Beck proposed 9 principles and 12 values that define the American experience. The principles are:

1) America is good.
2) I believe in God and He is the Center of my life.

---

[18] www.the912project.com

3) I must always try to be a more honest person than I was yesterday.

4) The family is sacred, my spouse and I are the ultimate authority, not the government.

5) If you break the law you pay the penalty, justice is blind and no one is above it.

6) I have a right to life, liberty, and the pursuit of happiness, but there is no guarantee of equal results.

7) I work hard for what I have and I will share it with who I want to, government cannot force me to be charitable.

8) It is not un-American for me to disagree with authority or to share my personal opinion.

9) The government works for me, I do not answer to them, they answer to me.

The 12 values are: honesty, reverence, hope, thrift, humility, charity, sincerity, moderation, hard work, courage, personal responsibility, and gratitude.

Outlining these guiding principles and values, Beck called upon Americans who share these beliefs to come together, meet up with others, and educate themselves on the philosophies of our country's founding fathers. Within a few days, tens of thousands of people had answered the call. Talk began about organizing a citizen's march on Washington D.C. for September 12, 2009.

———————————

Throughout the month of March, Tea Parties began to spring up in small towns, county seats and state capitols across the nation.

On March 7th in Fullerton CA local talk radio hosts John Kobylt and Ken Champiou of KFI-AM Los Angeles sponsored a massive rally. Eschewing the civil sounding name "tea party", they held what they preferred to call a "Tax Revolt 2009" event. Although more a mixture of carnival and AM radio program promotion, the rally was attended by an estimated 10,000 people angry over California's $20 billion budget deficit. John and Ken lampooned both the Republican Governor, Arnold Schwarzenegger, and prominent lawmakers in the Democrat controlled legislature.

That same day in Green Bay WI, outside the Titletown Brewing Company over 1,200 tax protesters gathered and listened to speakers including WTAQ talk show host Jerry Bader. "Conservatism is based on I'll take care of me, you take care of you." stated Bader. "This is often translated to mean we're not compassionate, nothing could be further from the truth. Picking my pocket and deciding what's compassion, is not compassion. When you are forced to be compassionate at the barrel of a gun, we have a word for that — it's robbery." The rally ended with the protesters marching to the downtown Green Bay office of U.S. Representative Steve Kagen (D-WI).

Local Tea Parties continued to spring up across the country throughout the month of March and into early April. Everyday Americans organized the Tea Parties: professionals, small business owners, and stay-at-home moms. They all shared a passion to "do something" to demonstrate their anger at state and federal elected officials who routinely dismissed their objections to ever increasing taxes and wasteful spending.

The movement was self-organizing and growing.

The Tea Parties became the forum of choice for the silent majority. However, their impact was limited and still under the radar of the establishment press and elected officials. Many realized a national day of widespread demonstrations was needed to raise the profile of the rallies to a level that could not be ignored. With tax day looming, Wednesday April 15th was the natural pick for a nationwide, same-day tax protest.

A coalition of Internet-based organizations formed to coordinate a new website, "Tax Day Tea Party", designed to serve as a central point for organizers to post information about their city's rally.[19] Hundreds of organizers began to use this site to register their intentions to hold rallies in their hometowns on Tax Day. The FreedomWorks website posted a map of the United States displaying each city planning a Tax Day Tea Party, with more virtual "flag pins" being added every day.

In the weeks preceding Tax Day, rallies attended by five hundred to a thousand people were held in such diverse locations as Santa Barbara CA, Naples FL, and Kalispell MT. Throughout these first weeks of the movement various individuals, taxpayer groups, talk show hosts, and websites continued to help the novice organizers obtain permits, broadcast information about the rallies, and reported on the turnouts.

---

[19] Eric Odom from the Dontgo Movement (American Liberty Alliance), Jenny Beth Martin from Smart Girl Politics, Adam Waldeck on behalf of American Solutions, and Michael Patrick Leahy representing #TCOT.

As April 15th dawned, the Tax Day Tea Party (TDTP) website had registered rallies in 850 cities and towns across America. Hundreds of other last-minute rallies were also held that were not registered at TDTP. The total number is unknown, however estimates run as high as 1,800 separate events across the country.

Local area residents procured their own site permits, arranged for speakers, prepared their programs, provided for public amenities, and promoted the events themselves. These were average Americans who had little or no previous experience organizing a large public event.

The response was tremendous and unprecedented.

The greater Atlanta metro-area hosted many local events. Early in the afternoon a group gathered at Roswell Square. WSB-TV Atlanta reported from the protest, capturing some comments from participants. "In the first place," stated Betty Givings, "I don't believe you can throw taxes at the situation we're in now. I think you have to work it out from the ground up." Catherine Watkins said, "I'm not as much against the taxes as I am against how they spend the taxes."[20]

Another late afternoon rally was held in Marietta GA at the classic town square in the historic center of the town. Jim Jess, a board member of the Georgia Tea Party (Mr. Jess speaks only on his personal behalf) reported, "I saw some familiar faces. But, also a lot of new faces." He continued, "As the event began, between 600 and 800 people had gathered, and a bugle sounded as a horse

---

[20] As reported by WSB Atlanta website on April 15, 2009: http://www.wsbtv.com/news/19184851/detail.html

and rider arrived announcing that everyone should beware: 'The taxes are coming, the taxes are coming!'"[21] Several hundred folks from this location boarded five buses and headed down to Atlanta.

Ultimately a surge of 20,000 citizens would swamp the Georgia State Capitol in Atlanta that Wednesday night. It was the largest Tax Day Tea Party in America. Georgians flew American and "Don't Tread on Me" flags, and some came dressed in colonial era costumes, both sights becoming familiar at the larger Tea Parties. A couple with three young children held a sign stating "Our Children – Our Future", while a man wearing a 101st Airborne Veteran cap had a sign asking, "Got Freedom?" One group held a bed sheet reading, "Capitalism Not Socialism – Enough – Stop Rewarding Failure".[22]

A major interest of Tea Party participants is the U.S. Constitution: learning about it, understanding it, and restoring it. The Atlanta event distributed 12,000 copies of the document; yet fell short of demand when the supply ran out.

Jim Jess tried to maneuver through the throng on Washington Street, which borders the State Capital on the west, to reach Martin Luther King Boulevard. Unable to make his way, he instead stepped up on a two-foot-high wall, joining a number of other folks who were already standing there. It gave him an "excellent view" and he remained there for the entire event.

---

[21] As reported on Examiner.com "Tax Day Tea Party and the birth of a new political movement – Part 1" by Jim Jess, April 16, 2009: http://www.examiner.com/x-7422-Cobb-County-Conservative-Examiner-y2009m4d16-Tax-Day-Tea-Party-and-the-birth-of-a-politcal-movement-Part-1
[22] As photographed by ATL Photographers and displayed on their website on April 16, 2009: http://atlphotographers.com/general/photographs-of-the-atlanta-tax-day-tea-party/

"I had attended many political events and rallies in the past, but there was something different about this crowd and the level of sophistication of the participants." stated Jess. "The liberal media will say that the Tea Parties were just a group of people with a grudge about paying their taxes. They will say that participants were being used by Republicans to make Obama look bad." Jess continued, "I humbly disagree. What is going on here is not just a 'rant' about taxes being too high or dissatisfaction with who won the White House. It's about policy. It's about the future. It's about citizens regaining a sense of connection with the political process. It is new in character and scope, and it will reshape American politics as we know it."[23]

A professional photographer present at the Atlanta event wrote on his website, "Let me start off by saying this was quite possibly one of the best rally/protests I've seen in my lifetime." He continued, "It wasn't an anti-Obama rally, or an anti-government protest, or a right-wing free for all. No, it was something much, much bigger than all the petty name-calling and nonsense. This was a true patriotic stand against a government that has gotten out of hand with its spending, taxation, and general Big-Brother ways."[24]

In San Antonio, an estimated 15,000 plus Texans poured into the Alamo Plaza, a rally that rivaled Atlanta in size. Although the event began in the afternoon, the protesters stayed well after

[23] As reported on Examiner.com "Tax Day Tea Party and the birth of a new political movement – Part 1" by Jim Jess, April 16, 2009:
http://www.examiner.com/x-7422-Cobb-County-Conservative-Examiner-y2009m4d16-Tax-Day-Tea-Party-and-the-birth-of-a-new-politcal-movement-Part-1
[24] ATL Photographers website on April 16, 2009:
http://atlphotographers.com/general/photographs-of-the-atlanta-tax-day-tea-party/

dark. The Plaza was thick with the personal messages of the patriots, "I Am Not the ATM for the Government" and "If I Can Keep My Guns, Money, and Freedom—You Can Keep Your Change."

The featured speaker was Doug Phillips, President of Vision Forum Ministries. During his speech titled, 'Freedom at Risk', Phillips declared, "The federal government is not our nanny. The federal government is not our mother. The federal government is not our doctor. The federal government is not the high priest of a new religion, and the federal government is not our savior!" He continued, "We were endowed by our Creator, not by the tree god, by our Creator, with inalienable rights. We are meant to be a free people. Message to Washington D.C., if you want our guns, our businesses, our Constitutional freedom," Phillips thundered, "come and take it!"[25]

At the California State Capitol in Sacramento 5,000 rallied to protest an upcoming special election on proposed state tax hikes. The Howard Jarvis Taxpayers Association was a co-sponsor and co-coordinator of the Sacramento Tax Day Tea Party. One protester had small American and Gadsden flags attached to each of the upper corners of his sign, which read "Tax His Teleprompter" and displayed the Obama campaign logo. Another sign expressing a popular sentiment read, "You Can't Fix Stupid—But You Can Vote It Out!"

The Sacramento crowd's favorite chant became "Vote Them Out", and it erupted frequently during the speeches.

---

[25] You Tube video of Doug Phillip's speech:
http://www.youtube.com/watch?v=q095smotEaw

During the rally Meckler pointed out that the Chairman of the California Republican Party, Ron Nehring, was at the gathering. The crowd responded with boos that resounded against the Capitol building to signal their anger at the state GOP for originally supporting the tax measures.

Featured speakers at the Sacramento rally were U.S. Representative Tom McClintock (R-CA), in recognition of his long Don Quixote-like fight against overspending during his time in the state legislature, and Michael Reagan, talk show host and son of former President Ronald Reagan. Michelle Malkin was also in attendance and was interviewed by Neil Cavuto, of Fox News, during his broadcast.

Across the country thousands gathered in White Plains NY, Kansas City MO, and Denver CO, while hundreds of citizens rallied in Carson City NV and Dayton OH.

The Dallas Police estimated "thousands" gathered in that iconic Texan city. One man held aloft a sign declaring, "I Want My Country Back!" with the letters USSA circled with the diagonal slash through them, and an American flag hand-drawn in the lower left corner with the words "America the Free!" The *Dallas Morning News* quoted participant Becky Hanshaw, who drove 10 hours from McAllen TX to be at the event because "it's time to stop the craziness." Hanshaw stated, "I work too hard to give my money away. This is a message to both parties, because I don't believe the Republican Party is conservative enough."

One of the larger rallies in Texas was held at Fort Worth's LaGrave Field, where 4,500 taxpayers heard Republican Governor Rick Perry. He urged Washington to cut spending and taxes, and reread the Constitution. "They're overturning the rights we had one by one, making choices that would leave our founding fathers scratching their heads."

In Illinois, between 6,000 and 10,000 Chicagoans descended on the downtown area. The Federal Plaza was packed to capacity, making it difficult to keep building entrances and sidewalks clear. The Chicago speakers included WLS 890 talk radio host Erich "Mancow" Muller, and Jonathan Hoenig, author of "Greed is Good: The Capitalist Pig Guide to Investing."

One large banner proclaimed, "IN GOD WE TRUST, Obama and Congress, Eh…Not So Much". A blonde little girl in a powder blue jacket held a sign she had colored with crayons reading, "Tomorrow Belongs to Me! I want to be free! Please don't enslave me with your taxes!" Another sign held by an even smaller girl asked, "How many zeros in a trillion? 1,000,000,000,000". Other signs displayed the messages, "Restore The Republic", "Grow Business, Not Government" and "Born Free, Taxed To Death"—with the 'x' in 'taxes' replaced with the communist hammer and sickle.[26]

In the wider San Diego area there were seven separate Tax Day Tea Parties, with an aggregate total of 10,000. In Oklahoma City OK, thousands packed the lawn in front of the State Capital, and the California Central Valley town of Fresno rallied over 5,000. Other cities included San Francisco CA, Grand Rapids MI, and Eau Claire WI.

---

[26] As posted on the website Surge USA on April 15, 2009: http://www.surgeusa.org/actions/tea/il_chicago_041509.html

In Charleston SC, young cadets from the Citadel were prominent participants. Among the crowd of native Charlestonians was Pam Dashiell, in the city from her home in western North Carolina attending a WTA Tennis Tournament. Dashiell relayed, "It was my first Tea Party. I had seen information online that there would be a gathering to protest the Obama Administration's agenda to tax and spend our lives into historic debt. The mainstream media there had predicted that perhaps 200-250 people might show up for the rally, but as usual, they underestimated the crowd of 3,000 that spilled out from the steps of the Commons House into the downtown streets."[27]

The Sioux Falls SD gathering featured a "tea dumping" reenactment in a local park's small lake, with ducks swimming past the scale version of an 18th century trading ship. Wearing colonial clothing, several men simulated dumping tea overboard to the obvious approval of the crowd.

Hundreds of Montanans showed their grit in Bozeman by rallying in snowy weather, while several thousands gathered in Lafayette IN near Purdue University. The only known Tea Party actually held on a college campus happened at the University of California, Merced, with 400 attending. Over 1,000 came out after dark in New York City, and in Boston MA, the home of the original Tea Party, 500 rallied.

April 15, 2009 became the largest, single day, multiple-city rally across the nation in the country's history. The Tax Day Tea Party website estimated the total nationwide turnout for their

---

[27] Pam Dashiell: Electronic mail interview June 21, 2010.

850 registered rallies at 1.2 million people.[28] This participant count does not include the hundreds of impromptu rallies known to have occurred that went uncounted on the national web site. Estimates by bloggers for unregistered rallies range between 500 and 1,000. Assuming 800 other rallies averaging 625 in attendance, it would not be presumptuous to add another half million to the national total.

On Tax Day, approximately 1,700,000 citizens rallied at Tea Parties across America to join in voicing their collective call for the government to stop spending, lower taxes, and repeal onerous regulations. They rallied to send a forceful message to their elected representatives that they were deeply concerned about the direction these public servants were taking the country. Each one of these Americans who went to a rally represented many, many more who share the same worries about losing liberties, and the same frustration towards politicians who refuse to do the people's will. They understand the very Constitution of the United States of America is in peril.

---

[28] 1.2 million divided by 850 averages 1,412 per rally.

Chapter Two

The Media:
The Fourth Estate as Fifth Column

"He that will promote discord,
under a government so equally formed as this,
would join Lucifer in his revolt."
- Thomas Paine, "Common Sense", 1776

Edmund Burke, the eminent British politician of the early 19ᵗʰ century, in an address to Parliament coined the term "Fourth Estate" as a reference to the press. Prior to the French Revolution, France's representative body was known as the Estates General. The members of the First Estate were the clergy, the Second Estate were the nobility, and the Third Estate were peasants and commoners. Some years after the French Revolution, Burke looking up at the Press Gallery as he addressed the House of Commons is credited as saying, "Yonder sits the Fourth Estate, and they are more important than them all."

Later in the century, the English wit Oscar Wilde wrote, "In old days men had the rack. Now they have the press. That is an improvement certainly. But still it is very bad, and wrong, and demoralizing." He continued, "Somebody — was it Burke? — called journalism the Fourth Estate. That was true at the time no doubt. But at the present moment it is the only Estate. It has eaten up the other three. The Lords Temporal say nothing, the Lords Spiritual have nothing to say, and the House of Commons has nothing to say and says it. We are dominated by Journalism."

During the Spanish Civil War the insurgent general Emilio Mola originated the term "fifth column" in a 1936 radio address as his forces, consisting of four columns, were marching on Madrid. He stated that a fifth column of radical supporters inside the city would help undermine the republican government from within the populace. The term has come to refer to any group who clandestinely undermine a nation from the inside.

The establishment media has increasingly and progressively become out-of-touch with mainstream America with their biased reporting. They give glowing reports of Democrat policies and their criticism is reserved for initiatives from Republicans. If a Democrat politician is involved in a scandal there is no mention of his party affiliation, but if the politician is a Republican his party affiliation is part of the headline.

Democrat presidents are presented as intelligent, thoughtful, morally upright, and compelling speakers. Republican presidents are presented as dumb, ignorant, immoral, and butchers of the English language. Liberal candidates' backgrounds are never fully investigated and reported, but a conservative candidate is subjected to microscopic inspection of every thought, word, and association.

The establishment media exhibits daily their unwavering support of Progressive ideologies, policies, and politicians. That support is manifested by their slide into being a propaganda vehicle for the radical left's relentless attempts to destroy the Constitution. Through their selective reporting and bias, the establishment media have become a fifth column undermining our society from the inside.

For decades the establishment media, comprised of major city newspapers and the three television networks (ABC, CBS, and NBC), had a monopoly on deciding what news to, or not to, broadcast to the American people. They were the force that shaped public opinion. That began to change in the late 1980's with the advent of talk radio. The repeal of the "Fairness Doctrine" by the Federal Communications Commission in 1987 allowed radio stations to air political opinion programs without the onerous requirement to give equal free time to any and all viewpoints. CNN offered 24-hour news programming and began to compete with the "Big Three" networks. Other 24-hour news channels followed including Fox News, MSNBC, and CNBC.

Beginning in the 1990's, the opportunity to disseminate information over the Internet put the "news" into the hands of everyday people. The number of Internet sites specializing in current political events grew exponentially, and became an alternative for people seeking out more details and opinions than those afforded them by the establishment press.

Without cable television, talk radio, and the personal computer, the actions by ordinary Americans holding a tax protest rally would never have grown beyond a one-shot local event. Wide dissemination over the Internet of the first tax revolt protests in February, coupled with the countless postings of "Rick's Rant", inspired regular citizens to organize themselves outside the bounds of the traditional political parties.

———————————

Fox News ran stories on the planning of the first Tea Parties after "Rick's Rant" and showed video of the Washington D.C. rally on February 27th. They also broadcast from the annual Conservative Political Action Conference (CPAC)[29] held in D.C. on that same weekend. Rush Limbaugh, a featured speaker, commented that he thought the Tea Party was a great idea.

Prior to the Tax Day Tea Party there was little print media coverage of the rallies, except for *Investor's Business Daily*, the *Christian Science Monitor*, the *New York Post*, and some local newspapers. Neither the establishment print nor television media covered the February or March events. However, new-media Internet sites and conservative talk radio reported them.

On February 20th David Hogberg, with *Investor's Business Daily*, was the first establishment reporter to cover the sprouting movement. Hogberg noted that the size of the tax revolt protests were "a far cry from the left anti-globalization and anti-war demonstrations of the past decades, but they appear to have grassroots origins".

He quoted Robert Borasage, co-director of the Campaign for America's Future and co-founder of the Apollo Alliance, a Progressive organization funded by the Tides Foundation and one of the worlds richest men, George Soros. Borasage, trying to downgrade the importance of the Tea Parties, said, "These protests are probably ideological rather than practical."

---

[29] CPAC is sponsored by the American Conservative Union, Young America's Foundations, and *Human Events* newsweekly. The annual conference has been held since 1973.

Patrik Jonsson of the *Christian Science Monitor* attended the Tea Party rally in Atlanta GA on February 27th, and accurately reported the outrage at both the political parties and the entrenched Washington elite. He wrote, "Many of the protesters expressed a sense that basic American freedoms of life, liberty and the pursuit of happiness are threatened by new Washington policies seen by many as more socialistic than capitalistic."

Jonsson concluded his reporting with this round-up of other events that day, "In Tampa, two-dozen protesters held up handwritten signs with slogans like 'Keep Your Bailout; I'll Keep My Freedom'. About 300 people showed up in 25-degree weather in Wichita, Kansas. In St. Louis, local media expected 50 people to show up while actual turnout surged to over 1,000 people."

On February 29th the *New York Post* covered a "mock tea party at City Hall Park yesterday," bringing out about 150 taxpayers. Organizer Kellen Guida, 26, was quoted, "I know my basic economics, and know the stimulus package doesn't work. [Obama] is going to add more to the federal deficit in 20 months than Bush did in eight years."

The *New York Post* also ran an editorial portraying the motivation of the participants. "The spark for most of these events has been a federal spigot pouring out money like a broken fire hydrant in August: bailouts for banks, automakers and home mortgages; a $787 billion stimulus; adding insult to injury, a $3.6 trillion budget."

The editorial continued, "The 'Taxpayer Tea Party' movement may not go anywhere, but it sure gives overtaxed, tapped-out folks a place to let off a little steam. At the same time, that 1773 tea party energized more than a few people, so who knows where this one might go?"

Michael Silence, of the _Knoxville News Sentinel,_ blogged, "Call it what you will, but conservatives organizing protests is something unheard of in recent times. That it happens at all with conservatives is a huge story. We expect the left to be generating these kinds of things. Not the right."

Several weeks before the Tax Day events, producers for various Fox News television shows began to contact individual organizers to ascertain where the largest rallies were likely to happen across the nation. Mark Meckler, now acting as the California state coordinator, was one of those called. "I was contacted by the producer of _"The Neil Cavuto Show"."_ Meckler explained, "She was interested in the largest event planned for the west coast to coincide with Neil's show (3:00 p.m. to 4:00 p.m. EST)." Meckler told her that Sacramento would be one of the largest and she expressed that there was potential interest. Similar calls were being made to Atlanta on behalf of _"The Sean Hannity Show"_, and to San Antonio for _"The Glenn Beck Show"_. Fox was trying to determine if the events were truly news.

"It wasn't until about ten days or so before the event that they finally said they were coming," said Meckler. "I encouraged them to come and cover the event. Knowing that most media outlets were ignoring us, I thought this was a way to get the message out." Believing they had a major news story on their hands, and indeed a "scoop" since no one else was reporting it, Fox promoted their own shows that were covering the rallies.

Fox News television programs followed the Tax Day Tea Parties across the time zones beginning with the rally in Sacramento CA with *"The Neil Cavuto Show"*, moving to the Alamo in San Antonio TX featuring Glenn Beck and rocker Ted Nugent, and wrapping up with Sean Hannity covering the after dark gathering in Atlanta GA. The rallies featured speakers and live music, and lasted between three and four hours at each location. Fox News broadcast only the portion of a city's protest coinciding with each particular program.

Fox program hosts interviewed organizers and participants, included wide shots of the crowds, and zoomed in on the personal messages displayed on the homemade signs. Fox News fairly reported the motivations of both organizers and participants, allowed viewers to observe the deportment and excitement of the crowds, and captured the new zeitgeist emerging in American politics.

The establishment media coverage of the Tax Day rallies was marked by either dismissal of the Tea Parties' importance, or were pointedly hostile, derisive, and perverted.

The most infamous report came from CNN reporter Susan Roesgen covering the Chicago rally. She began her coverage by singling out a man carrying a sign detailing the reasons he believed President Obama was a fascist. She proceeded to argue with him, plaintively asking, "Why be so hard on the President?"

Later, the website Newsbusters reminded readers about a 2006 rally against then President George W. Bush where a protester was wearing a large Bush mask complete with a colored-in Hitler mustache and red horns attached to the forehead. In that report, Roesgen said, "But while a look-alike showed up with a wad of cash, Mr. Bush did not." Instead of angrily confronting that protester she used him as a prop for her report.

Roesgen continued her coverage from Chicago pointing out various signs held by the protesters and reading their messages in a voice dripping with disdain. She approached a young father holding his toddler. In response to Roesgen asking him his reasons for being at the rally, he began to quote Abraham Lincoln but was rudely cut off by Roesgen who asked, "But what does that have to do with taxes? Don't you know that Illinois will receive stimulus money?" People nearby began to shout at her, "Let him speak!"

Pandering to the camera, Roesgen commented that the event was "anti-government", and "anti-CNN" because it was "highly promoted by the right-wing conservative network Fox" and "not really family viewing." The crowd responded with chants of "Liberal Bias" and "CNN Go Home!"

After the CNN camera was turned off, a woman participant questioned the reporter's obvious bias and dismissive remarks. The exchange was caught by another tea partier with his camera. Roesgen adopted an uncharacteristic child-like demeanor and asked the woman innocently how she came to know about the Tea Party if not through Fox. The exacerbated woman responded, "It's all over the Internet!"

The clips of Roesgen's report and the later confrontation were posted on the Internet, replayed by the new-media outlets across the country, and by anyone with a web connection.

CNN was bombarded with outraged phone calls and later had to shut down Roesgen's email inbox. The next day CNN announced that Roesgen would be taking a break from the network. In the next few months she only appeared to report on the Drew Peterson[30] arrest and the death of entertainer Michael Jackson. On July 17th the network announced that Roesgen's contract would not be renewed.

On April 15th the "Big Three" network news shows spent most of their time downplaying the grassroots and non-partisan nature of the events, their significance, and even disagreeing with the tea partiers about their stated reasons for participating.[31]

Dan Harris of ABC reported, "Cheered on by Fox News and talk radio, the hundreds of tea parties today were designed to protest the bailouts, the stimulus plan, and President Obama's budget. But critics on the left say this is not a real grassroots phenomenon at all, that it's actually largely orchestrated by people fronting for corporate interests. While the Boston Tea Party in 1773 was about taxation without representation, critics point out that today's protesters did get to vote, they just lost. What's more, polls show most Americans don't feel overtaxed."

Harris also unquestioningly reported, "The White House says the president is unaware of the tea parties and will hold his own event today."

CBS's Dean Reynolds noted that a Tea Party organizer "insisted these events were non-partisan, but a fistful of rightward

---

[30] Drew Peterson, a suspect in the disappearance of his fourth wife, Stacy, was arrested on May 8, 2009 for the murder of his third wife, Kathleen Savio.
[31] As compiled and reported by Newsbusters: http://newsbusters.org/blogs/seton-motley/2009/04/20/summary-april-15-tea-parties-media-coverage

leaning websites and commentators embraced the cause." Reynolds then proceeded to repeat the tax meme, "It's important to keep in mind that fresh polling indicates there is not all that much passion about high taxes in the country at large right now. Gallup this week found 61% of Americans see their federal income taxes as fair."

Over at NBC, Lee Cowan reported that "organizers insist today's Tea Parties were organic uprisings of like-minded taxpayers from both parties," but "some observers suggest not all of it was as home-grown as it may seem." The "observers" turned out to be NBC News White House reporter Chuck Todd, who stated, "A lot of sentiment is about organizing anti-Obama rallies, getting conservatives excited about the conservative movement again."

Cowan later commented on the public sentiment, "Although today's organizers called this national day of protest a success, polls show that a slim majority of Americans actually approve of the bailout plan. What they disagree with is where the money should go."

On NBC's *"Today"* show, Todd wrote off the protests saying, "There's been some grassroots conservatives who have organized so called 'tea parties' around the country. But I tell you, the idea hasn't really caught on."

MSNBC had actually started their Tea Party bashing early on with the April 13th broadcast of David Shuster's comments featuring a term for oral sex that had previously been unknown in the common American lexicon.

Shuster sneered, "For most Americans, Wednesday, April 15th will be Tax Day. But in our fourth story tonight: It's going to be tea-bagging day for the right wing and they're going nuts for it. Thousands of them whipped out the festivities early this past weekend, and while the parties are officially toothless, the tea-baggers are full-throated about their goals. They want to give President Obama a strong tongue-lashing and lick government spending, spending they did not oppose when they were under presidents Bush and Reagan. They oppose Mr. Obama's tax rates, which will be lower for most of them, and they oppose the tax increases Mr. Obama is imposing on the rich, whose taxes will skyrocket to a rate about 10% less than it was under Reagan. That's tea-bagging in a nut shell."[32]

Later that day on "*The Rachel Maddow Show*", both Maddow and liberal talk radio "Air America" host Anna Marie Cox picked up on Shuster's thinly veiled reference and repeated the term "tea-bagging" at least 51 times in a thirteen-minute segment. On April 14th, during a report by senior political analyst David Gergen commenting that Republicans really had nothing to offer, CNN anchor Anderson Cooper interjected "tea-bagging, tea-bagging". When Gergan closed by saying that Republicans were "searching for their voice" after two electoral losses, Cooper quipped, "It's hard to talk when you're tea-bagging."

During the April 15th coverage, CNN reporters Jeffrey Toobin and Christiane Amanpour gave voice to their skepticism

---

[32] As compiled and reported by Newsbusters:
http://newsbusters.org/blogs/seton-motley/2009/04/20/summary-april-15-tea-parties-media-coverage

about the Tea Parties, with Toobin stating how it was "disturbing" that there was an "edge of anger at the government" at the rallies.

He continued, "There is a real, real hostility that is not just politics as usual among some of these people. I think its indicative of trying to tap into an anger that's beyond rationality on a part of a small group of these people." (If any gentle reader can translate this 'thought' into a coherent sentence, please advise author.) Amanpour asked if the protesters weren't "really out of step with the majority of Americans."

MSNBC coverage sank even further during the April 15th broadcast of *"Countdown with Keith Olbermann"*. Before Olberman introduced actor/activist Jeneane Garofalo, he stated, "Congratulations, Pensacola tea-baggers. You got spunk. And despite the hatred on display, few of you actually violated the penal code. But tea-bagging has now petered out, 'taint what it used to be. And when you co-opt the next holiday, Fourth of July, try to adopt a holiday food that does not invite double entendres, like, you know, franks and beans." Olberman then transitioned, "On a more serious note, we're now joined by actor and activist, Janeane Garofalo."

"Thank you," Garofalo opened. She continued emphatically, "You know there is nothing more interesting than seeing a bunch of racists become confused and angry at a speech, they're not quite sure what he's saying. It sounds right to them, and then it doesn't make sense. Which, let's be very honest about what this was about. It's not about bashing Democrats, it's not about taxes. They have no idea what the Boston Tea Party was about. They don't know their history at all."

Then she snarled, "This was about hating a black man in the White House. This is racism, straight up. That is nothing but a bunch of tea-bagging rednecks."[33]

What happened at the Pensacola FL Tea Party to inspire such fury?

After the program of speeches and music ended, the organizers announced an "open mike" and invited any of the estimated 500 participants to make their own comments. A self-described Progressive took the opportunity to address the crowd. He opened his remarks by honoring the service of veterans, current service members and gold star families, with the crowd cheering those sentiments.

He then stated that there was a budget surplus in 2000, but it was "destroyed by the profligate spending of the Bush administration". The crowd began to get restless. He then asked the folks to cheer if they made less than $250,000 a year, and after the prompted uproar, he commented, "Your taxes are going to be cut under the current budget. Congratulations!" He continued, "I was laid off in September because my employer had to make budget cuts. That was before the election, okay? So let's remember, that if you're going to argue about more taxes and less spending, to place the blame where the blame belongs, and that's squarely in the hands of the Republican congress until 2006 and the Bush administration."[34]

---

[33] Ibid.
[34] As posted on Daily Kos website:
http://www.dailykos.com/storyonly/2009/4/16/720820/-Yeah,-Im-the-guy-who-spoke-at-the-Pensacola-Tea-Party

The crowd responded with robust booing.

Pensacola citizens were called racists on a national cable "news show" because, when this man attempted to deflect the responsibility of the current situation to the Bush administration, he was booed.

The thirty-something, out-of-work lawyer, immediately became a minor celebrity on the Progressive blogs. The Daily Kos posting of his story, under the name "Sinfonian", was picked up by Newsvine, and heralded under the cumbersome title, "One Brave Soul Tells The (Many) Pensacola Teabaggers Who Make Less Than $250K That Their Taxes Are Being Cut Under The Obama Administration". Newsvine posters gushed, "That takes guts," and "I'm really surprised someone had the nerve to do what he did. I like his style."

A conservative poster rebutted this sentiment beautifully. "No guts needed," opined "Seabhac Re", "when a liberal stands up in a crowd of centrists, libertarians, and conservatives, he/she can say what they want without fear. They may get booed, but that's about it. However, imagine a conservative standing up at a liberal protest rally (Seattle '99) and trying to 'teach' them their view of history. Now that would take guts as well as good medical insurance."

On April 29th Reason Magazine Online featured an article by Matt Kibbe, President of the FreedomWorks Foundation, titled "Stages of Denial – Take Pity on the Left as It Grapples with the Tea Party Revolt." Kibbe had attended the April 15th Atlanta GA event.

55

Kibbe wrote, "Judging from the left's hysterical reaction something really big must have happened. But the only way to really understand the left's misinformed and paranoid attacks is to realize that the protests represent tangible proof that basic libertarian values continue to resonate with the American electorate. That, apparently, is a difficult thing for some to accept." His favorite sign of the day was "Give Me Liberty, Not Debt".

"Call me old school", he continued, "but I still live in a country where the citizens more than 'value' their liberties and their ability to express opposition to government policy. These liberties define us; they bind us as nation. They are explicitly defined in the Constitution and Bill of Rights. So make fun of me. Call me a 'tea-bagger', if you must."

"Did the tea parties matter?" he asks, and answers, "One reasonable measure of progress may be the sheer volume of vitriol produced by their critics. This alone is an attractive value proposition." He observes, "I don't believe that the official Republican apparatus can effectively organize these voters for 2010. Indeed, the very nature of the tea parties defies top-down direction. The protests, just like the free market process they tacitly espoused, were decentralized and driven by voluntary action."

He concludes, "Who knows, next November those protesters might just show up to vote against the politicians who dismissed the tea party revolt of 2009 as 'Astroturf'."[35]

---

[35] As posted on Reason Online April 29, 2009:
http://reason.com/news/show/133177.html

The nation's major newspapers did their best to ignore the Tax Day Tea Party, or reported data and poll results to dismiss the intent of the events. Only the *Washington Times* reported a straight news story.

The *Washington Times* story ran on April 16th. "Online Efforts Boost Tax Day 'Tea Parties'", by Jennifer Harper, described the importance of the Internet and social media outlets in organizing the national endeavor.[36]

"We know the mainstream media is not going to offer a full range of coverage," Harper quoted Roger Simon of Pajamas Media. "Citizen journalism can do it better. We've got 500 people reporting in using CelleCast, a service where they can report with voice, photos and videos over cell phones. It goes online within 30 seconds." Pajamas Media is the home to many conservative bloggers, such as Instapundit, and has a sister television network PJTV.

USA Today in its April 16th issue gave nine paragraphs on page 3A under the headline, "Thousands Rally at 'Tax Day Tea Parties'" by Oren Dorell. The article spoke briefly about the gathering outside the White House, while reporting in more detail on the Lansing MI appearance of "Joe the Plumber" before a crowd of 3,000 to 4,000. "Joe the Plumber" became famous for asking, during the presidential campaign, then candidate Obama about his economic policies. In an unguarded moment Obama answered that he believed we "should spread the wealth around", to which Joe, replied, "That sounds like socialism."

---

[36] The Washington Times, April 16, 2009:
http://www.washingtontimes.com/news/2009/apr/16/online-efforts-boost-tax-day-tea-parties

Reporters pointedly observed that his real name was not "Joe" but Samuel Joseph Wurzelbacher, and within days Mr. Wurzelbacher's tax history was leaked to the press in a pathetic attempt to discredit him and deflect attention from Obama's comment.

The *USA Today* article quoted Joe at the Lansing rally as saying, "I came here today to have my voice heard. I'm going to keep working, calling my senator, my congressman. The more your voice is heard, the more actual change that can take place." The article mentioned rallies in Kentucky, Salt Lake City, and Sioux Falls. It also quoted Eric Odom from the Liberty Alliance, who said, "Most of the people who showed up today were not involved politically [before] in their lives."[37] However, the previous day's issue featured a front-page article, six times as large, insisting that "Most Americans OK with Big Government, At Least for Now."[38]

The *New York Times* published their first report of the nationwide Tea Party movement with a short article by reporter Liz Robbins titled "Tax Day Is Met With Tea Parties", on page 16 of Thursday's edition.[39] The article stated, "Although organizers insisted they had created a nonpartisan grassroots movement, others argued that these parties were more of the Astroturf variety: an occasion largely created by the clamor of cable news and

---

[37] USA Today, April 16, 2009:
http://www.usatoday.com/new/washington/2009-04-15-tea-parties_n.htm
[38] As compiled and reported by Newsbusters:
http://newsbusters.org/blogs/seton-motley/2009/04/20/summary-april-15-tea-parties-media-coverage
[39] Ibid.

fueled by the financial and political support of current and former Republican leaders."[40]

The *Washington Post* showcased a text box at the top of page one with a headline, "Tax Burden Near Historic Low". The D.C. Tea Party was noted at the bottom of the page and readers were sent to page B-1.[41]

The *Los Angeles Times* ran no stories about the Tax Day Tea Parties on April 16th. However, they ran an editorial on April 17th titled "Untangling Our Taxes" which mentioned the Tea Parties in passing. "Obama's gesture came as 'Tea Party' protesters held rallies across the country to complain that the administration's fiscal plans will force taxpayers up and down the economic ladder to part with more of their earnings. In response, the president touted the tax cuts already adopted for students, businesses and taxpayers making less than $250,000 a year."[42] (The "tax cuts" that were only changes to the withholding formula.)

An interesting column ran in the April 18th edition of the *Bangor Daily News* written by Kent Ward. He observed that while his paper ran pictures and stories of their local Tax Day Tea Party on the front page, inside the paper's Section B was an article listing some of Maine's "recent handouts from the federal government".

---

[40] New York Times, April 16, 2009: http://www.nytimes.com/2009/04/16/us/politics/16taxday.html?

[41] As compiled by Newsbusters: http://newsbusters.org/blogs/seton-motley/2009/04/20/summary-april-15-tea-parties-media-coverage. A search on the Washington Post website for the article yielded no hits.

[42] Los Angeles Times, April 17, 2009: http://www.latimes.com/news/opinion/editorials/la-ed-taxccoe17-2009apr17,0,301501

Ward wrote, "Our Washington sugar daddy had sent us $5 million to help reduce poverty; $3.3 million to stop terrorism here dead in its tracks; $423,794 for food pantries and homeless shelters; $363,000 for boating projects; and a request from the Environmental Protection Agency for the state to make a pitch for up to $35,000 available for 'green' projects in New England." Ward continued, "In any case, it was only one day's worth of government alms seemingly designed to get us hooked on handouts, like dopeheads hooked on heroin, with no prevailing concern in Washington that the bill will some day become due."

Regarding the general response of the media to the Tea Parties he stated, "My claptrap meter tells me that both camps may have been partially correct in their assessments. Which is more than could be said for House Speaker Nancy Pelosi. Not surprisingly, the polarizing California dragon lady dismissed the nationwide protest as more a bunch of rich people engaged in a group whine than a legitimate grassroots demonstration of anger with congress and the Obama administration."

Ward concluded, "My favorite [sign] was held by a young girl, perhaps 10 years old, one of the future taxpayers who will be picking up the tab, 'I Read As Much Of The Stimulus Legislation As Those Who Voted For It,' her sign proclaimed. Didn't we all."[43]

On the April 15th broadcast of CNBC's *"Squawk Box"*, co-host Joe Kernen asked Rick Santelli what he thought of being a "cultural phenomenon".

---

[43] The Bangor Daily News, April 18, 2009:
http://www.bangordailynews.com/detail/104024.html

Santelli told of his pride in the American people. "I don't know about cultural phenomenon, but I'll tell you what," Santelli responded, "I think that this Tea Party phenomenon is steeped in American culture and steeped in American notion to get involved with what's going on with our government. I haven't organized. I'm going to have to work to pay my taxes, so I'm not going to be able to get away today. But, I have to tell you, I'm pretty proud of this." Santelli continued, "I think from a grassroots standpoint, I'm sure some of the media out there is not going to peg it that way, but isn't it about as American as it gets for people to roll their strollers, and make their signs, and go voice their opinion about the direction of the country?"

"Good, bad or indifferent", he concluded, "that's a great thing. There's not a lot of countries, of course, that afford their people...that right. It' a great thing."

The influence of the establishment media in the shaping of American opinion has eroded in direct proportion to their inability to report the truth as they become further enmeshed in propping up the radical Progressive agenda. Limited in their own self-awareness, they continue to blame their loss of viewers and readers to the generalized boogeyman of the Internet. They are partially correct in knowing where their customers are going. However they do not, and perhaps never will, admit that their own shoddy and biased "news" reporting has driven their audience to seek out the new-media for timely and relevant information.

Just because a tree falls in the forest, and a Progressive has his hands over his ears, doesn't mean the tree did not fall. The initial reaction of the establishment media was to ignore the first tax revolt protests and early Tea Party rallies. When the Tax Day rallies were too huge to ignore completely, those who were forced to report on them did so in as demeaning a manner as possible. Totally oblivious to an honest expression of rational and deeply held concerns, the media elite insulted most of their audience and the American people.

Where the establishment media only reported on stories that were of interest to them, or that promoted the Progressive agenda, the websites, blogs, radio talk show and conservative cable television hosts filled in the gap. Citizen journalists joined their efforts to track and report a display of watchful citizenship never before seen on the American political stage.

As their fifth column bias and tactics became more pronounced, an ever-increasing number of Americans found the establishment media to be irrelevant. Rather than relying on the media elite for information, citizens began to use the new-media sites on the Internet and added their own voices to the public debate.

The silent majority is silent no more.

Chapter Three

The People:
Silent Majority – Silent No More

"O ye that love mankind!
Ye that dare oppose, not only the tyranny
but the tyrant, stand forth!
Every spot of the old world is overrun with oppression.
Freedom hath been hunted round the globe.
Asia, and Africa, have long expelled her.
Europe regards her like a stranger, and England hath given
her warning to depart.
O! Receive the fugitive, and prepare in time
an asylum for mankind."
-Thomas Paine, "Common Sense", 1776

The American experience for the average working person, usually a "card-carrying" member of the silent majority, has always been to provide for their families, to be active in their churches and communities, and to rely on their elected officials to take responsible care of the business of government. Since the early years of the twentieth century the country's governance has been slowly moving away from the Constitutional system designed to uphold the power of the individual, to a federal bureaucracy controlling nearly every aspect of its citizens' lives through burdensome taxes and excessive regulations.

In the book *"Liberal Fascism"*, Jonah Goldberg traces the 100-year incremental adoption of statist[44] ideas and policies within all levels of government and significant sectors of our culture. Goldberg documents the legislative efforts, by both political parties, that have taken power away from the private citizen and put it into the hands of elite policy makers and faceless bureaucrats. These efforts were often cloaked with fine sentiments to "help the common man", but the real consequences of these polices rendered larger and larger numbers of individuals dysfunctional and dependent upon government for the needs of daily living.

Socialism manifested itself in America at the turn of the 20th century with the Progressive Movement, and was popular with people in both political parties. Both President Teddy Roosevelt, a Republican, and President Woodrow Wilson, a Democrat, embraced Progressivism. It was their policies that saddled American citizens with the Federal Reserve Bank, the prohibition of alcohol, the League of Nations/United Nations, and the "progressive" income tax and the establishment of the Internal Revenue Service. All Progressive policy initiatives undermine private property and wealth, impose restrictions on personal freedom, and support a government run by an elite intellectual class dictating to the "unwashed masses" how to live.

Slowly over the course of the last century, those who envisioned a top-down run utopia began to construct an alternative governmental structure that was the antithesis of the United States Constitution. Woodrow Wilson began to lay the foundation of the

---

[44] The distilled totalitarian agenda shared by the political philosophies of Marxism, Socialism, and Progressivism.

Progressive state during the First World War, Franklin D. Roosevelt poured the cement and built the first floor with the New Deal, Lyndon Johnson completed the second, third and fourth floors with the Great Society, and various gingerbread and filigree work has been added by subsequent Democrat and Republican administrations. All aided and abetted by money-corrupted congresses populated by career politicians. The resulting structure is more reminiscent of the Winchester Mystery House[45] than Mount Vernon.

As the decades slipped by, the great silent majority living the traditional American values of hard work, honesty, and love of home and country, felt increasingly uncomfortable about the growing power of the federal government and viscerally knew something was not right. They just had no name for it.

There was one brief shining respite for the average citizen with the presidency of Ronald Reagan. Many conservative and libertarian bloggers refer to Reagan as "Ronaldus Magnus". With his sincere American optimism he connected directly with the people who shared his belief in the greatness of America, in her freedoms, and in her Constitution. The establishment press savaged him constantly, and so despite his great efforts, at best he succeeded only in slowing the slide into socialism. Reagan once said, "You can tell a communist because he reads Marx and Lenin, you can tell an anti-communist because he understands Marx and Lenin."

---

[45] The Winchester Mystery House in San Jose CA, was built by the daughter of the inventor of the Winchester rifle. She felt she had to continue construction on her house to appease the spirits of those killed by her father's invention. The structure is known by its dead-end hallways, doors that have no rooms, and secret passage ways.

65

After the humiliation of Jimmy Carter's inept handling of the Iranian take-over of the American Embassy in Teheran, with our hostages being held for over 400 days, Reagan led the nation into a new era of pride, patriotism, and prosperity.

Conversely, the subsequent congresses and the administrations of George H.W. Bush, Bill Clinton, and George W. Bush, continued to build an ever more unresponsive and repressive federal system that encroached upon the liberties of the common man.

Barack Obama won the presidency, by a bare majority 53% of the vote, based on gauzy promises of "hope and change" that would move the country into a new "post-racial" era. He promised an administration free of lobbyist money and influence, and transparent legislation without wasteful spending. The appointment of powerful lobbyists to important administration positions, and the rushed approval of the Stimulus Bill soon gave lie to these empty promises.

During the campaign, and up to the present moment, Obama's core political philosophy has been glossed over by a compliant establishment media. They never reported any statements from his past that would give evidence to his Socialist/Progressive-based political ideology. Such as his appearance on Chicago Public Radio for a 2001 interview, where then Illinois State Senator Obama explained his belief that the Constitution needed to be radically reinterpreted to allow for the redistribution of wealth.

Obama began, "If you look at the victories and failures of the Civil Rights Movement and its litigation strategy of the Court, and where it succeeded was to vest formal rights in previously dispossessed peoples." He continued, "But, the Supreme Court never ventured into the issues of redistribution of wealth and served more basic issues of political and economic justice in this society. And to that extent, as radical as I think people tried to characterize the Warren Court, it wasn't that radical."

Elaborating further he explained, "It didn't break free from the essential constraints placed by the founding fathers in the Constitution, at least as its been interpreted. And the Warren Court interpreted it in the same way—that generally the Constitution is a charter of negative liberties, says what the states can't do to you, says what the federal government can't do to you, but it doesn't say what the federal government or state government must do on your behalf."

He then laments the continued existence of these "essential constraints placed by the founding fathers" upon our government by stating, "And that hasn't shifted and one of the, I think, tragedies of the Civil Rights Movement was, because the Civil Rights Movement became so court focused, I think there was a tendency to lose track of the political and community organizing, and activities on the ground, that are able to put together the actual coalitions of power through which you bring about redistributive change, and in some ways we still suffer from that."[46]

Obama's interpretation of the Constitution is diametrically opposed to the intent and purpose of our founders.

---

[46] WBEZ.FM Chicago Public Radio, 2001. You Tube video:
http://www.youtube.com/watch?v=NTCNK7v3J6w

The establishment media has been complicit with Obama in misrepresenting a political agenda that intends to destroy our Constitutional Republic. They are also unwilling to ask key questions about his suppressed educational records, friendships, and associates. They accept blindly, and dare not to define more closely, what he meant by proclaiming, just prior to his inauguration, "We are within five days of fundamentally transforming the United States of America".

The Progressive left, now controlling the Democrat leadership, were emboldened by their capture of the White House. Coupled with their majority in congress, they began to push their radical agenda. Within the first few months of the new administration, a growing number of Americans became horrified at the avalanche of huge bills, averaging 1,000 pages plus, that came tumbling down on them from a congress too bent on amassing power to even read the legislation before voting for passage. Massive and sweeping legislation seemed to be dropping from the sky, each bill marked "urgent", and each in turn imposing stifling regulation on banking, industry, energy, and even personal health care.

The tipping point had been met.

Led by the example of the first tax revolt protests, the silent majority began to use the last few weapons left them—their voices and their presence in the street. They began to recognize that the old Democrat-Republican dichotomy was a distraction, and they realized the true battle lines lie between the people and the Progressive politicians of both political parties. If freedom and liberty were to survive in the United States they needed to be vigorously defended, and defended now.

It was as if the country had fallen over a cliff and the end of the lifeline was just a few feet from disappearing off the edge itself. Some quick thinking Americans grabbed that line and others, recognizing the danger, joined them and began to pull. Every time a member of the silent majority joined a Tea Party protest, another American gave hand to that lifeline.

The first Tea Party organizers and participants instinctively understood the importance of keeping the movement focused on lowering taxes, stopping spending, and lifting oppressive regulation. At the heart of the movement is the conviction and intention that no sitting politician, neither Democrat nor Republican, shall be safe from censure if their actions fail to support these basic ideals, no matter how eloquently they express empty focus group words to their constituents. Declared party affiliations by registered voters are declining. The percentage of voters who define themselves as Independents has risen from 30% to 39%, while Democrat registrations have declined from 39% to 33%, and Republican registrations have dropped from 26% to 22%.[47]

Many Tea Party organizations do not request elected officials to speak at their rallies, but cordially invite them to participate. The novel notion being that the people have been listening to politicians for years, so it is now time for politicians to listen to the people. Any elected officials who are invited to speak

---

[47] As reported by Fox News, July 17, 2009

generally have long track records of fighting for limited government, lower taxes, and personal freedom.

New grassroots movements are often co-opted in their infancy by opportunists attracted by any sizable crowd. The first challenge for many neophyte Tea Party groups throughout the country was to keep the movement non-partisan. The experience in Little Rock AR is indicative of how front-line Tea Party people respond to these situations.

Charlie Johnson, a 72 year-old retired Captain from the Little Rock Fire Department and former small business owner, inadvertently found himself an organizer for the local Tax Day Tea Party.[48] While looking up TDTP on the web for information about the movement, he "somehow clicked the wrong button and bingo, I'm an organizer", he remembered. "I thought it over after realizing what I had done and thought that maybe this is what I was called to do, so here I am today, up to my neck in Tea Party business."

"Tax Day was held in front of the Arkansas State Capitol Building in Little Rock," wrote Johnson. "To everyone's amazement we had 2,800 folks show up on a very hot afternoon. Some with homemade signs, some with American flags, some in costume and some just came to talk with us, but all were mad and ready to show our non-representing representatives we are not happy. Sadly we had very little press coverage and only a couple local politicians. But that has changed now-a-days."

The second national Tea Party day was scheduled for the Fourth of July. Again, a natural choice for a day of protest against

---

[48] Charles E. Johnson: Letter of August 17, 2009.

the anti-American policies of the Progressive left. However, in Little Rock another organization called Little Rock Tea Party Inc. had arrived on the scene. They wanted to forgo the Fourth of July date and instead hold the next big rally on June 15th, the state holiday of Arkansas's Birthday. They appeared to have a large on-line base and were well-organized, so local Tax Day organizers, like Johnson, put their energies behind the June 15th rally.

"The rally was billed as a fund raiser with food, music and speakers and not really as a protest," wrote Johnson. "I think because of that a lot of people were put off and we had only around 600 attend." He continued, "Then on stage one of the organizers of Little Rock Tea Party Inc. announced his candidacy against Senator Blanche Lincoln and that he would be running on the Republican ticket. A couple other State Representatives announced their intent to move up the food chain in local politics also."

Johnson and others from the original Tax Day rally talked later and "felt like we had been kind of ambushed by this organizer, because we had always stated we were non-partisan folks who were just mad and wanted things to change." Due to this incident, the grassroots Tea Party group lost support from some of the original organizers. The Republican organizer of Little Rock Tea Party Inc. eventually stepped down, and a core grassroots group reformed and continues to grow. "My wife and I have joined a small group just getting well-organized in Benton AR, a small town 20 miles west of our home that has a large

71

number of like-minded Christian folks, and where we felt we could better serve."

Johnson is dedicated to seeing a restoration of traditional American values in our government. "I feel the importance of the Tea Party Movement strongly, and I plan to keep working for a real change. My hope is that a conservative candidate that I can whole-heartedly support will come out of this by then. The founding fathers never considered anything other than part-time politicians and I think we need to return to that."

Johnson's testament is that of a purebred American citizen activist. Openly and honestly he chronicles the widely shared experience of Tea Party people. The calling is heartfelt and the commitment to the cause is bedrock solid. Obstacles or difficulties are only learning experiences and are to be overcome by independently motivated action.

————————————————

Another early challenge for the emerging national movement came from established groups that wanted to include social issues as part of the Tea Party agenda. Many veterans of the various battles of the culture war were naturally drawn to the Tea Party Movement because all of their important concerns shared a common source, the Progressive radical left. The major issues of the culture war include abortion, euthanasia, homosexual "marriage", and illegal immigration, just to name the top four.

The novice national and local Tea Party coordinators wisely recognized that the Progressives had long used social issues as a divisive tool. If participants were to advocate for various social issues, the cohesiveness and focus of the Tea Party Movement would be distracted from the core issues of fiscal responsibility, constitutionally limited government, and a free market. Tea Partiers know the success of the Progressive agenda means the elimination of traditional Americanism by a transformation into some imitation "new republic", bearing no resemblance to the America of our founders. If the Constitution could not be conserved, the ability to even discuss social issues would be no more.

After the tremendous success of the Tax Day Tea Party, Amy Kremer, Mark Meckler, Jenny Beth Martin, and other organizers knew the Tea Party movement was not going to fade away. It was obvious that it had harnessed the power of the American spirit. Within days the Tax Day Tea Party website was renamed Tea Party Patriots and began an open solicitation for submissions, comments and position essays to articulate the core ideals, values, and strategies of the Tea Party Movement. Amy Kremer became a national coordinator, as well as Mark Meckler and Jenny Beth Martin. Others continued organizing on the regional, state, and city levels. They built a web center to keep up with the bombardment of legislation, facilitate nationwide rally days, and feed the growing movement with information.

The silent majority had finally found the answer to their despairing question "What else can I do?" and that answer filled them with courage, resolve, and determination. They answered the call from patriots past and present, and as they came out with their signs, everyone was astonished at the number of same-minded citizens joining together.

Elijah Condellone, a young father, first became involved as a Tea Party participant at the St. Louis Tax Day Tea Party held at Keiner Plaza.[49] Condellone stated, "Estimates from the police department ranged between 5,000 and 6,500 people."

For the past five years Condellone had been becoming more involved in grassroots efforts and "figuring out how I stand on issues". He continued, "My interest in the political landscape really began after I had children. That put things in perspective."

Condellone started the Alton IL Tea Party organization when he returned home from the April 15th St. Louis rally "after seeing so many like-minded people". He continued, "It takes a lot of time, but I do what I can do. I still have to work full time."

Alton's first Tea Party was held on July 25th. Police estimates put the crowd at 2,200. Condellone's favorite sign that day read, "Free to Succeed, Free to Fail, Free to Choose". (The "too big to fail" argument was used to justify the government bail out of the banks and automakers.) Condellone commented, "It's on you to succeed or fail, but you have to work to succeed and not just get handouts. It's not about what you deserve. We need to get away from the entitlement mentality, the entitlement society that both political parties give us. Government is providing for people what they should provide for themselves."

"There were young people, older people, and middle age," he declared. "All walks of life and many registered Democrats. We have to get past this party affiliation and get back to what is best for the country, not the party." His view of the current state of our two political parties is stark. "The Democrat Party is a mere

---

[49] Elijah Condellone: Telephone interview on August 6, 2009.

74

shadow of itself, of what it once was. The Republican Party may be salvageable, but people are disappointed in both. We are not concerned with party politics. We are concerned about preserving our Republic and our free society in the USA. If the [political] parties want to get on board, that would be fine."

To preserve the core non-partisan nature of the Tea Party movement, no politicians speak at Alton rallies. "I know this is true for the St. Louis Tea Party as well. It's about the American people voicing their opinion and people willing to fight to preserve our freedoms. We believe in conservative values of limited government, as outlined in the Constitution, a tax structure that supports the private sector, no government expansion, and representatives who support us."

"We don't have a representative government now," Condellone continued. "Elected officials need to understand they work for us. We have elitists so disconnected from what average Americans have to go through, and they are not affected by their policies. Things need to change."

He shared some observations, "What I am seeing now with the Tea Parties is the American people starting to wake up. Like the Japanese Admiral Yamamoto said after bombing Pearl Harbor, he was afraid they had awakened the sleeping giant. Well the sleeping giant of the American people is stirring. People are saying that things are just not right."

"The government is pitting people against people," he stated. "They are rewarding doing nothing over being productive because the more you make, the more they take. People get money for doing nothing productive for society."

Condellone continued, "This is not the country, values, or work ethic in which I was raised. My family served in the military. Sorry to say I did not, but my father was a Viet Nam vet, and I had seven great uncles who fought in WWII, one was on Iwo Jima."

He concluded, "I was raised to love the history of this country, and to love the capitalism that supported our free society. This is not what we see today or the country our children will grow up in. It's like George Orwell's "*1984*", left is right, up is down, right is wrong."

Another active member of the Alton Tea Party is Ken Russell, who got involved because "my wife knows Elijah."[50] He continued lightly, "She held me at gunpoint and told me I was volunteering. So I did."

On a more serious note, Russell explains his reasons for getting involved. "Marxists controlling the House [of Representatives], a filibuster proof Senate, a Marxist in the White House, a left leaning court, ACORN (Association of Community Organizations for Reform Now), SEIU (Service Employees International Union), AmeriCorps, 32 czars, and GOP leadership who fall down, roll over and soil themselves each and every time Reid, Pelosi and Chris Matthews whispers 'boo' in their ear. How else are normal Americans going to have a voice?"

He displayed the depth of his concern for our country with a cynical comment, "We are on an afterburner ride away from personal and national relationships with God. Now, if you'll

---

[50] Ken Russell: Electronic mail interview on August 4, 2009.

excuse me, I have to find out more about Michael Jackson and the next American Idol season. Has Britney [Spears] cured her cellulite problem?"

His sarcasm continued regarding the role and impact of talk radio on the Tea Party Movement. "Well, you know we're all highly paid by Big Talk Radio and Big Health Insurance, and therefore could never do any of this on our own. We're 'stupidly' and bitterly clinging to our guns and Bibles, and eating road kill so much how could we know what to do unless talk radio told us?"

Russell concluded, "It's not the same country I grew up in nor the same country for which I served in the Marine Corps. Last January, I woke up in a different country and I am trying to find out if the United States is missing behind the what-not shelf."

Margie Sorbi has been to two Tea Party rallies.[51] "I'm a patriot. I'm 74 years old," she stated proudly. "I heard about the Tea Party movement back in March and knew it was a great thing. I went to the Tax Day Tea Party in Santa Rosa CA." No neophyte here. "I've been aware of this stuff for twenty-five years. I sign petitions, write elected officials, and give donations when I can to groups who are fighting for America," Sorbi said.

A long time observer of the political scene, Sorbi remarked, "This movement has exploded because the radicals have over-extended. Barack has gone too far, too fast. People have just been sleepwalking, but this over-reach is too much."

---

[51] Margie Sorbi: Telephone interviews on August 13, 2009 and September 26, 2009.

77

"The elected officials want power. They use communist tactics to tear us down, like porn on TV. These are the tactics of evil. We are in a spiritual war, and people are vulnerable to spiritual attacks and they don't even know it." (Pornography diminishes the inherent nobility of the individual, as participants become the object of base pleasure for the illicit profit of others. It shatters the beauty of the physical union between a husband and wife, and replaces it with a sex act that is mechanical and devoid of attachment. "Free love" has long been a staple in the collectivists' toolbox used to break down traditional marriage and stable family cohesion.)

"Look at the kids in school," she continued. "If I had kids now I wouldn't let them within a mile of a [public] school. I would teach them at home. I give some home schooling moms a break and teach Spanish to their kids a couple of hours a week. You can sure tell the difference between home schoolers and those that go to public school. Sad to look at most kids today because they are totally lost."

An avid listener of conservative talk radio, her favorite hosts are Glenn Beck, Mark Levin, Michael Savage, Bill O'Riley, and Rush Limbaugh. "They have been very helpful to the Tea Party movement, but they did not instigate it. They have supported it and free speech." Concerned about anticipated new "local diversity" rules that may come down from the Federal Communications Commission, she declared, "If all the radio hosts were taken off the air, I think I would run outside and start hollering, 'Follow me to change this!'"

78

Her greatest concerns for the country include, "Loss of our sovereignty, freedom and Constitutional rights. We'll become a communist nation and then global government. If we fail, there may be a revolution. People will have to be ready to defend themselves." The Second Amendment to the U. S. Constitution states, "…the right of the people to keep and bear arms shall not be infringed." Experience has taught Sorbi to hold dear her Second Amendment rights.

"I defended myself once in 1974 from an attack from a man I knew. He wanted to have sex with me and I said no. I protected myself with my hand gun." Chuckling a little, she recalls his reaction when he saw her with the gun; "I was standing in my bedroom when he came in. He stopped, looked, and asked, 'Is that for real?' and I answered, 'Yes, its real.'" As she cocked back the hammer she stated firmly, "I know how to use it and I won't hesitate." He just said, "I guess you're the boss now."

Sorbi relayed that she had driven alone across the country for several weeks in 2002. When someone asked her neighbor if she had gotten on the road all right, her neighbor answered, "Yup. When she left she had her dog, her Bible, and her gun."

In early April, Gordon Rupp held a 9.12 Project meeting at his home.[52] Someone who attended apparently gave his name to Mark Meckler. "A few days later I was contacted by Mark," Rupp remembered. "He asked me if I would agree to be

---

[52] Gordon Rupp: Telephone interview on August 10, 2009. Electronic mail correspondence on August 26, 2009 and October 4, 2009.

interviewed by a local TV station to explain what a Tea Party was. The interview was at 6:00 a.m., live from Weber Point (the site of the April 15th event). Boy, was it cold!" Rupp continued, "After that interview we were off to the races with only a couple of weeks time to coordinate the Stockton area for the Tax Day Tea Parties."

"The motivating factor for me was the Stimulus Package." He continued, "It was the final straw. The representatives are no longer listening to us. Our phone calls are just flushed. They walk lock-step with the administration, whether it is Democrat or Republican."

With just two weeks to organize, Rupp pulled together the April 15th Stockton rally. A crowd of 450 attended. "We got a lot of spillover from Sacramento because ours was scheduled for 5:00 p.m. We haven't garnered the same numbers as April 15th, but on the Fourth of July we had 150, and on July 17th we rallied at two of Jerry McNerney's (D-CA) congressional district offices. At the Stockton office we only had 18, but at the Pleasanton office we had 170. We are a small group but growing every day." (On July 17th Tea Party Patriots held another national day of rallies in front of senate and representative district offices.)

"I've been doing all this myself," Rupp stated. "Although I have been getting some help in answering the emails and returning phone calls." Rupp's group came up with an innovative idea to broaden the awareness of the Tea Party Movement. They decided to host a 'meet and greet' table at Banner Island Ballpark for the game between Stockton and San Jose. Rupp explained, "This was an effort to reach out to folks that don't own a computer or are not Internet savvy. People are clamoring for information."

"We did have to pay a fee to rent the table," Rupp relayed. "I needed $300. I put out some emails and had the donations in just a few hours." They chose August 21st because it was Boy Scout—Girl Scout Night, so they knew there would be many family oriented people coming to the game.

Rupp reported, "Since I have been in this movement there has been quite a learning curve on crowd types. We got the good family values crowd we were expecting, but the other side of the coin was parents coming in the gates, getting the free giveaway for the kids, finding the seats, then marching back to buy the hot dogs, soda and chips. That left little time to visit our booth. They did, but time was limited."

"So we ventured out into the crowd," he continued, "and passed out our handouts. We did get to talk to many, and those we did talk to were in agreement with us, and what we were doing. We did not encounter anyone that was in disagreement, but I am thinking that if there was, that this was not the place to engage in a heated debate. There were those that saw us and then would not make eye contact."

Rupp experienced something unexpected, "I was surprised by the amount of teenagers that did talk to us and had a positive opinion on what we were doing, which could be a reflection on their upbringing." Speaking of his newfound insights, Rupp said, "Having a booth at a Tea Party, street fair, or an event in a park would probably be more productive because of the ability to talk to people in a laid back environment. I learned that was not possible in a ball park full of kids!"

"On the other hand," he observed, "we did get our name and movement exposure I wanted, including getting our name posted on the outfield scoreboard and mentioned over the P.A. system. My main goal was exposure to Stockton and that is what I got." Rupp stated, "Everyone in our whole group had the same ideas, but no place to go to meet with like-minded people. Then we go to a Tea Party rally and find out there are other people who feel the same way. I knew on April 15th I had arrived and had someone else to share my thoughts."

When asked if the Tea Parties are making an impact, Rupp replied, "Yes, but they (elected officials) are still not conceding defeat, just making excuses rather than facing the truth. There is no money for the health insurance reform they are proposing. And now they are bringing in the union thugs." Rupp observed, "This is just helping bring others into our groups."

Another self-starter in the Stockton area is Jean Sadler[53]. "I made up fliers, placed them at church, my medical facility, my grocery store bulletin board. A lady that had contacted me by email copied my flier and gave it to her children to hand out to teachers at their respective schools. I left these fliers everywhere I went for two weeks." Sadler emphasized, "We were not an angry mob. We did not wear Brooks Brothers suits, we were in jeans, t-shirts and shorts." ("Brooks Brothers suits" refers to a comment by Senator Barbara Boxer (D-CA) on the August 4, 2009 broadcast of the MSNBC political show "*Hardball*": proffering as proof that the opposition displayed by citizens to Obama's health care plan was an organized

---

[53] Jean Sadler: Electronic mail interview on August 6, 2009.

diversion, she said that the participants are "wearing Brooks Brothers suits and too well dressed".)

Sadler continued, "We had blacks, whites, East Indian, and Hispanics. Cars were passing us on their way home from work, honking and giving us the thumbs-up sign, and waving in support of us. Some did stop, get out of their cars and joined us." She jokingly continued, "I don't know…maybe there *were* some Brooks Brothers suits amongst them!" Of the experience, she commented, "I was pleased and amazed. There were children, seniors, and middle age people. It was a wonderful event to see so many same-minded people in one spot."

"We are sick of this government encroachment on our personal lives." She continued, "We don't want government to adopt socialized medicine, Cap and Trade, higher taxes, and bigger and bigger government. We don't trust the czars [of] this administration. In California our farmer's crops are burning up due to some dang fish that the environmentalists want to protect. We were the 9th largest economy, and now we are bankrupt and burnt up!"

"We are a small town, Stockton," she concluded, "but we have loud voices and they will join with the many."

———————————————

Linda Dorr is a breast cancer survivor.[54] "I'm glad I got treated before government healthcare takes over." Despite being a busy small design business owner, she "spends two plus hours on Tea Party Patriots per day."

———————————————

[54] Linda Dorr: Telephone interview on August 19, 2009, and electronic mail September 25, 2009.

After attending the March 7th rally in Fullerton, sponsored by John Kobylt and Ken Champiou of KFI-AM Los Angeles, Dorr decided to become a Tea Party organizer for her home-town of Laguna Beach CA.

They held their first rally on Tax Day with over 500 participants. They also rallied on July 17th outside of Congressman John Campbell's (R-CA) office. Dorr emphasized, "I do this on my own time and with my own money."

"The silent majority is silent no more," declared Dorr. "Even Democrats are so opposed to what is going on. There is no longer time for people to just stand by and watch while they transform this country."

She recounted that their rallies drew a mixture of political party affiliations, "they are not all Republicans." She continued, "I've never seen anything like this in our country. Folks from all walks of life that love this country saying, 'We don't want our freedoms taken away!'"

Dorr acknowledged that citizens had "been asleep at the wheel, but they are not asleep any longer." She commented, "Strange friendships are developing among the people. We may conflict in our political leanings, but we agree on this."

Commenting dryly she said, "The media doesn't cover us. Fox does some. But, we're going ahead." She concluded, "Americans are heroes. We are the ones that saved whole countries, and now they are turning against the Greatest Generation, the WWII vets and their wives."

Besides the two major political parties, people are also fed-up with the alternative parties. Gail Lightfoot, a retired Registered Nurse, is the County Central Committee Chair for the local Libertarian Party in San Luis Obispo CA.[55] She has been a registered member in the Libertarian Party since 1972, active since 1980, and has run as a candidate eight times.

"As the years have gone on," Lightfoot stated, "the newer leaders of the Libertarian Party think that if they look and act like a major political party that, someday, somehow the media will see them as a major political party. I and other Libertarians, who are more reality oriented, grow discouraged." Lightfoot continued, "We (Libertarian Party) are not big, we are not powerful, we do not have the money the two parties in power have and we certainly cannot pass out favors. In order to succeed the 'other' parties have to [have] grassroots local activists fighting for self rule, self control and independence."

The first Tea Party she ever attended was the one she organized for Tax Day. Replying to a question regarding attendance she quipped, "About 100 people I did not know before that evening, myself and four friends." She continued, "The local newspapers covered us and gave us a front page photo."

Due to realities on the ground, Lightfoot planned the Independence Day Tea Party rally for Friday evening, July 3rd, "because the crowds on the 4th would bury us and have us stuck in traffic trying to get home again." Lightfoot held the event at a park visible from U.S. Highway 101 to "get the public's attention".

---

[55] Gail Lightfoot: Electronic mail interview on August 7, 2009, and electronic mail September 20, 2009.

Thirty others joined her on that busy holiday weekend. "Americans are finally mad about government action they don't think is right." She then added, "About time, too!"

"There are nearly as many reasons to get involved as there are people," Lightfoot continued, "illegal immigration, Stimulus, Cash for Clunkers (actually perfectly good cars), religion, weary of the race card being played over and over again, seeing government abuse, law enforcement abuse, misuse of power, ignoring the wishes of the people. More and more Americans are beginning to see the danger of too much 'other control' of their lives. At least I hope so!"

To Lightfoot the greatest concerns facing the country are "the clear and continuing violation of the Constitution until 'we the people' have no way to stop the government from its illegal activities; loss of the little bit of free enterprise left to us; and the lack of knowledge on the part of our citizens." She elaborated, "Most Americans have no clue as to what freedom really is, what it means and how important it is to advancement. Certainly they know nothing about the free market or that we lost it long ago, or that government intervention is the problem not the solution."

"In reality," she opined, "to win this war against entrenched politics, we have to use guerilla tactics." She continued, "I decided that we needed to cross party lines or ignore them, to find the people who recognize the problem and are ready to do something about it. We ended up with a Tea Party."

Lightfoot started a monthly Book Club, and began to hold a Tea Party once a week. "The pressure must continue, otherwise the politicians in power will all be re-elected and nothing will really change at all. I dread a take-over of the discontented by 'people in power' who will talk the talk without walking the walk at all. There is a hue and cry about what is happening and I really, really wish it could lead to less 'other' government and more 'self' government."

Michael Williams is a college senior in Georgia, who carries a double major, and the attendant double course hours.[56] He first heard about the tea parties on talk radio, but was already actively involved even before the spot fires flared. "On Election Night, 2008," he remembered, "I made the decision that the only way to reverse the trend and re-take the congress in 2010 was for every one of us to begin reading, learning, and self-educating."

Serious in his endeavor, he explained, "I began buying books by my favorite talk radio hosts, and then I moved on to the books they cited as their sources. For Christmas that year, instead of asking for video games like every other year, I only asked for a few shirts I could wear to work, and a two-foot tall stack of books."

"My involvement with the Tea Party Movement really started there," he observed. "If I had not been studying and self-educating for several months, I probably would not have been ready for the opportunity when it was presented to me."

---

[56] Michael Williams: Electronic mail interview October 19, 2009.

Williams found out about the Atlanta Tax Day Tea Party from *"The Sean Hannity Show"* on Fox News, and decided he was going to attend. Within a few hours he was on the Atlanta organizer's website, "I saw that they were looking for volunteers to organize pre-rallies in various counties in the metro area. I decided I could probably lend a hand. The next day I received a phone call asking me to come to a meeting that weekend."

After working the local pre-rally in Cobb County, and the 20,000 strong rally at the Georgia State Capitol on Tax Day, Williams continued his activities with the local Cobb group and attended events throughout the metro Atlanta area. It did not take long before others noticed this energetic young man. Following the July 3rd event, he was invited to become a member of the Board of Directors of the Cobb Tea Party. "After we determined that we had attendees from every congressional district in Georgia, we changed our name to the Georgia Tea Party."

In addition to working with three nearby Tea Party groups, he is involved with the North Georgia 9.12 Project, We The People Revolution, Grassroots in Action PAC, and FreedomWorks. Williams also delivers speeches on the Tea Party Movement to various community groups. "The purpose of these speeches is to clear up the misconceptions about the Tea Party Movement proliferated by the media."

"My greatest concern," he continued, "is that our young people are being indoctrinated by the Left. I will be graduating this May with two bachelor's degrees, so I'm well aware of the tactics employed by liberal professors." He warned, "Their long term strategy is taking place in the classroom, and we need to do something about it before it is too late."

In regards to the impact of conservative talk radio and Fox News he opined, "They provide us with an outlet, that's all. We can rely on those sources to provide us with information that is not readily available. There are those who believe these sources are driving this movement, but I disagree. If anything, we're driving them."

When asked why he thinks the Tea Party Movement exploded across the country, he offers Thomas Jefferson's words in the Declaration of Independence, "...mankind are more disposed to suffer, while evils are sufferable, than to right themselves by abolishing the forms to which they are accustomed. When a long train of abuses and usurpations, pursuing invariably the same Object evinces a design to reduce them under absolute Despotism, it is their right, it is their duty, to throw off such Government, and to provide new Guards for their future security."

Williams qualifies his use of that particular quote, "Now, we are far from being reduced under absolute despotism, but I think the idea holds true. Ronald Reagan used to talk about the silent majority, the everyday American who works hard, pays his taxes, goes to church, and never bothers anybody else."

"When an administration gets under that majority's skin, however, they rise up and forever alter the direction of this country." He concluded, "That's all that's happening here. They've gotten under our skin."

For Donna and Phil Scott of San Diego CA there are "so many reasons to get involved."[57] Donna continued, "We are very concerned about too much government power, the radical Islamic Movement, higher taxes, and naïve American citizens for starters. The Tea Party was a perfect way to voice our opinions and carry out our forefather's traditions. Our country was founded on our Constitution and our First Amendment grants us freedom of speech. This has created the best and most free, up until recently, country in the world, and we wanted to show our support for the U.S. Constitution."

The Scott's first "Tea Party" was an April 8th letter-writing session sponsored by the local Republican Federated Women's group held at an area restaurant. Donna related, "Approximately 70 ladies and gentlemen spent one to three hours addressing envelopes and including tea bag tags. The Post Office had notified us that filled tea bags would not be delivered to any elected officials' office."

"We had great fun writing notes and sharing some of the familiar names we happened to draw." Donna quipped, "You can imagine the remarks when one of us would pull names like Nancy Pelosi, Joe Biden, or Barney Frank!" They received one reply. "A Republican congressman's assistant from Northern or Central California wrote a note stating that she was pinning our note and tea bag tag on their office wall."

The Scotts attended the Tax Day Tea Party in front of the Carmel Valley Post Office. "We read about the local Tea Party to

---

[57] Donna and Phil Scott: Electronic mail interviews on August 10, 2009 and September 20, 2009.

be held near our home. There was no official sponsoring group and it was purely grassroots," she emphasized. "Those of us who arrived a little early grouped together with homemade posters, American flags, 'Don't Tread On Me' flags and tons of enthusiasm. After our group grew too large, some of us spread out across the four corners of the intersection."

"This was an extremely busy intersection," Donna continued, "and the vast majority of passing motorists honked and gave us the thumbs-up sign. We would estimate 2,500 people were in our group and it was amazing because of the cold, windy weather. We had all ages, babies in strollers with signs pleading not to tax these youngsters, white haired citizens using canes and wheelchairs, teenagers, you name it."

"We didn't recognize one person from our Republican organizations. We discovered many registered Independents, Libertarians, and even Democrats, who were so sorry that they had voted for Obama. We had no clear-cut leader organizing the crowd, but there was no doubt about the strong views. It was an inspiring event!"

For the Independence Day Tea Party they attended an event coordinated by the North County Conservatives on June 28th at Grape Park in Escondido CA. Donna remembers, "The red, white, and blue decorated stage was set for a blue grass [musical] group, and many local conservative speakers. They had a huge copy of the U.S. Constitution hanging up and encouraged all of us to sign and write notes. This was going to Washington, D.C. The approximately 1,500 people were once again, all ages, all different party affiliations and all were American patriots."

She concluded, "What we found of interest was the local media inattention. The first letter writing campaign was not really reported to most San Diegans. The Carmel Mountain Post Office gathering was practically ignored by the local media, and the Escondido gathering had a little exposure on one of our smaller, less popular TV stations. I guess they are trying to ignore us so that we will go away. Or, is that the slant on the 'angry mob'?"

―――――――――――――

Jeff Jarvis of Ohio is not sure when he first heard of the Tea Parties, but he knows it was before April 15th. "The Tea Parties gave me more hope that people would 'wake up' sooner rather than later."[58]

"I got involved because I could," he continued. "I wanted to add to the numbers, even though I doubted a very large turnout in liberal Cleveland. Surprisingly, the first Cleveland event had over 2,000 in attendance. There were a couple of troublemakers, but they were run off by some fearless patriots." Jarvis attended the event on July 3rd, and "also the Tea Party Patriots event when Obama came to Cleveland to push his health care agenda."

Relaying his observations about the growth of the Tea Party Movement, Jarvis stated, "I don't think many people realized the extent to which a radical agenda would be implemented [by this administration]. Despite all the warning signs, the majority of people simply rested on their laurels or didn't vote. Now, a certain level of panic has set in and people realize that they better get off their asses and do something.

―――――――――――――

[58] Jeff Jarvis: Electronic mail interview on August 5, 2009.

Anything. There is a good deal of rational fear out there and good people are going to mobilize in an attempt to refute Obama."

Among the concerns Jarvis has about the state of the country are, "An economic downturn, the likes of which we have never seen." He elaborated, "We are already in uncharted territory with respect to government spending. This will not be quickly solved. Many people will look for the easy way out, and the taxpayer will be left with the tab. Anyone with a bit of sense could see that the sub-prime lending program was doomed from the beginning. Yet, many people continued to spend money they didn't have because it was so commonplace. It was painless."

Jarvis is a bit jaundiced about the impact of talk radio, "Certainly talk radio has fueled the movement. However, I wonder how many newcomers have been converted. I believe that talk radio is basically preaching to the choir." He concluded, "With the dearth of media coverage, growing the movement may be a daunting task. The media aren't reporting the news anymore. It's mostly agenda driven propaganda."

Michael Fincher is a co-founder of the College Republicans at the newest campus of the University of California in Merced.[59] He serves as the group's Vice President of External Affairs and Treasurer, and he is also a Senator in the Associated Students at the University of California, Merced (ASUCM) student government.

---

[59] Michael Fincher: Electronic mail interviews on September 15, 2009 and September 20, 2009.

Besides his college work, he reads widely in the conservative political genre: *"Liberal Fascism"* by Jonah Goldberg, *"Liberty and Tyranny"* by Mark Levin, *"Do the Right Thing"* by Mike Huckabee, *"Conscience of a Conservative"* by Barry Goldwater, and *"The 5,000 Year Leap"* by W. Cleon Skousen.

Fincher heard Rick Santelli's rant on the Internet and through emails from friends, and then learned of the Tax Day Tea Party online. "It was a good idea to protest the spending." He explained, "No one else was planning one in our area, and there is no real resistance to our Democrat representatives who are out of touch with local issues. We decided to hold a Merced Tax Day Tea Party on our campus, and open it to the whole community. We knew it would be hard to plan it in a short period of time off campus."

They held their first Tea Party on April 15th. He reported, "We estimate around 400 people being present at our rally at its peak – many people came and left throughout the day." They provided lunch for their guests consisting of over 30 boxes of pizza and dozens of cases of soda. They also offered for sale "iTeaParty in Merced" t-shirts, which sold out within minutes, and distributed copies of the Constitution and their publication *The Right Side*.

Various media outlets, including the local paper and TV news channels, covered the event. Fincher relayed, "It was funny to see people express their frustration of poor coverage and bias to the reporters, who found no way to explain themselves." He continued, "Our event, in our view, was a success, even though the number of attendees was less than other rallies, such as the Tax Day Tea Party in Fresno, where 7,500 showed up."

On July 3rd they held a second Tea Party that had a lower turnout of between 100 and 200 ralliers, featuring "community representatives who were fed up with the current situation." This event was held off-campus. "We learned planning an event on county property could cost you a fortune. We had to pay for permits, buy security, and we cancelled the free bbq since we would have to rent portable restrooms and meet other Health Department standards."

He believes the explosion of Tea Parties has occurred because, "People have been fed up, and after the Santelli outburst things snowballed into the current movement. We have put up with years of politicians putting us in debt, and the first rounds of Tea Parties were an awakening for many."

Regarding the role of talk radio he observed, "In the sense of Hannity, Limbaugh, and other national hosts, talk radio was an advertiser of the Tea Parties, but did not do much to support the rallies, or help the movement, like local less known radio shows. Most of the movement solely took place on the Internet." He continued, "In our wider area there were many Tea Parties being planned for the Fourth of July until the local radio station took control of it. Although I disagreed with them in holding one large rally, they did a good job." The reported attendance at the large single rally in Tulare (CA) was more than 10,000. Fincher explained, "The reason I disagreed with their viewpoint on holding just one is that their location was over 100

95

miles away, and my opinion was that fewer people would participate in one large rally than would participate if every town held one."

His greatest concern is, "That people will become complacent again, and that many will remain apathetic to the state of our country." He continued, "When I was in high school, they spent only a few days on the founding of our country in civics, and while in college I realized that many people, even 'educated' students, have absolutely no clue about how our nation was founded, and what the founding principles were. Most have no sense of the purpose of the Constitution, and do not factor in Constitutional restraints when forming their opinions on policy and politics."

Tea Party rallies continued to be held daily, weekly, and monthly in cities and towns across the country. Tea Party Patriots called for two nationwide rally days in July: Independence Day to celebrate liberty in contrast with the freedom-stealing legislation being passed, and July 17th to protest the health care plan outside congressional district offices.

The Independence Day rallies were spirited, despite the fact that many people were busy with family events and the turnouts were smaller than those seen on Tax Day.

After hosting the biggest Tax Day Tea Party in the nation, one major city was conspicuously absent from the July 4th lineup: Atlanta GA. The Atlanta Tea Party had begun planning their event in March, and chose the site of the old

Macy's building at the Gwinnett Place shopping mall. They had the permission of the building owner, had obtained all required permits, and had arranged for volunteers. However, just three weeks before the event they, along with the property owner, were called to a meeting with the mall manager. Simon Malls, founded by Melvin and Herbert Simon (large contributors to the Obama presidential campaign), owned the mall but not the old Macy's building.

Julianne Thompson, the organizer of the event, stated, "The manager told us Simon does not want political events on its property. They were also concerned about the fact we were using the term 'protest'." Thompson continued, "Although the event was on private property, the mall was able to assert authority on the matter due to reciprocal property easement agreements" pertaining to the use of the parking lot by mall patrons. (Odd, since the rally was planned to start late in the day when the mall would be closed, there would be no customers affected by any supposed impact on parking.) Disappointed, the organizers tried for the next two days to find a suitable venue for their rally, but were unsuccessful. They then directed Atlanta residents to attend events in their immediate areas.[60]

One of those local area events was held on July 3rd. It was sponsored by the Cobb Tea Party and held in Marietta's Jim Miller Park. Sheltered under a wooden pavilion decorated with clusters of red, white and blue balloons, 7,000 patriots came with their flags, banners and signs. The featured speaker was Herman Cain, a conservative talk radio host on 750 WSB Atlanta.

---

[60] Atlanta Tea Party website: http://www.atlantateaparty.net/

Blogger Michael Naragon on "The Constitutional Alamo" website stated tongue-in-cheek, "There's nothing like getting together with a bunch of tea-bagging rednecks to protest a black president, is there Janeane?[61] Oh, that's right you weren't there to hear that most of the night's comments were directed at Barney Frank and his comrades in congress, or that 'an angry black man' did most of the talking. Oh well, there's always September 12th".

Patriots held signs proclaiming their personal messages, "*We the people* Proud Owners of AIG+ GM", "Cap Gov Spending, Trade Congress", and "Capping Our Rights, Trading Our Freedom! Vote No!" Naragon commented, "Reminders (event posters and t-shirts) of the 15,000+ April 15th Atlanta Tea Party were everywhere, but no one seemed to mind the change in venue forced by the pro-Obama Gwinnett Place Mall. The Cobb Tea Party folks were very well organized, and the assembly came off like clockwork. In other words, it was very unlike Washington."[62]

The Dallas Tea Party, along with Smart Girl Politics, sponsored the largest rally in the nation at the famous South Fork Ranch in nearby Parker TX. Billed as "America's Tea Party" the event drew an enthusiastic crowd of 37,000. Beginning in the afternoon under triple-digit temperatures, the crowd swelled as the rally went on into the evening and after dark.

The signs had a definite Texas edge to them: "Got Common Sense? Texas Does" and "Republic of Texas...Soon". Others proclaimed, "King George Wasn't This

---

[61] Reference to Janeane Garofalo's comments April 15, 2009 on MSNBC's "*Countdown with Keith Olberman*" regarding the Pensacola FL Tea Party. See Chapter Two.

[62] As Reported on The Constitutional Alamo website, by Michael Naragon: http://theconstitutional/alamo.com/page/4/

Bad", "Dump Congress in Boston Harbor" and "I Was Tired of Yelling at My TV — So I Came Here". Speakers and live music kept the crowd entertained throughout the afternoon. Michelle Malkin was a featured speaker in the evening, and was followed by a Texas-size fireworks display.

The Dallas Tea Party also made a special video before the event inviting Janeane Garofalo to come to the rally "and learn the truth about who we are". The video featured many citizens: white, black, Hispanic, men and women, and even Michelle Malkin herself. Ms. Garofalo did not attend.

In Tucson AZ over 5,000 rallied to hear radio host Tammy Bruce. In a report on the Tucson Tea Party website, Trent Humphries wrote, "Our law enforcement officers told us that there was not a single disturbance. We were just a bunch of law-abiding citizens abiding the law. Wait, I thought we were right wing extremists."[63]

The "Freedom Rally Tea Party", held in the great Central Valley of California, saw a reported 15,000 at the Agri-Center in Tulare. "This is the most patriotic thing I could be doing on this 4th of July," stated participant Michelle Riddle. Another rallier, Adam Deis said, "We feel like we all have to speak with a very loud voice in order to be heard because we feel like we're being ignored."[64]

Santa Rosa CA held their rally early in the morning under overcast skies and a chilly 57 degrees. Approximately 400 patriots came together in the Old Courthouse Square to enjoy speakers, music and camaraderie. The organizers also had a series of tables

---

[63] Tucson Tea Party: http://www.tucsonteaparty.org/?m=200907
[64] KFSN Fresno, July 4, 2009:
http://abclocal.go.com/kfsn/story?section=news/local&id=6898346

representing the ten amendments of the Bill of Rights with a special learning activity for children. Among the personal messages displayed, "Even God Only Asks For 10%", "Wake the Sheeple", and "Angry and Disgusted — Read the Bill".

Among the many other cities holding Independence Day Tea Parties were Portland OR, Shreveport LA, Franklin TN, Boston MA, and Savannah GA. Over the extended holiday weekend, it is estimated more than 1,000 separate events were held throughout the country.

After congress returned from their Fourth of July recess, the Tea Party Patriots called for a national protest day on July 17th to focus on the health care reform bill. The Tea Parties were held at the same hour in all time zones, from 12:00 until 1:00 pm (EDT), outside senate and congressional field offices across the country. Amy Kremer, a national coordinator for Tea Party Patriots, reported that approximately 450 locations were involved with crowds ranging from dozens to hundreds. The response from district staff varied from meeting with the constituents and listening to their concerns, to hiding behind drawn blinds and closing the office.

In St. Louis MO at Senator Claire McCaskill's office, the staffers called the police. The over 100 protesters had to move from the sidewalk in front of the office to the street median. Approximately one hundred and fifty ralliers braved 115-degree temperatures in Palm Springs CA to protest in front of Representative Mary Bono-Mack's office. Bono-Mack was one of the eight Republicans to vote "yes" on the Cap and Trade bill.

Another 150 Tea Partiers lined the sidewalk in San Diego CA outside the building that houses offices for Democrat Senators Diane Feinstein and Barbara Boxer. One hundred came together in Raleigh NC, and 200 lined both sides of the street in Napa CA outside Democrat Congressman Mike Thompson's office.

Obviously, this was a new experience for the field offices. One can just imagine the phone calls that were placed to the elected officials in the nation's capitol. President Obama responded late that Friday afternoon with an unscheduled press conference during which he touted the benefits of nationalized health care, but refused to answer any questions.

The Tea Parties were becoming a thorn in the side for the president and his Progressive minions in congress. Career politicians were being forced to counter the message of the patriotic citizens, even if those same officials refused to publicly recognize the existence of the rallies or the legitimate concerns expressed.

At the heart of the Tea Party movement is the desire of citizens to restore the Constitution as the working framework for our government. The citizen's concerns are not unfounded, and their desires are not frivolous. The discrediting charge—that the Tea Party movement is as artificial as Astroturf—coming from entrenched politicians and the establishment media, appeared to citizens to be disingenuous criticism. On April 18, 2009, Speaker Pelosi had scoffed that the Tea Parties were "Astroturf" politics to protect the "wealthiest of Americans".

Having relied so long on "community organizers" within their network of radical left organizations, Progressives could not draw a crowd any other way. Since they had become so immersed in this method, they assumed everyone else had to do the same things, and measured their opponents by their own synthetic standards.

Generally, Astroturf demonstrations by Progressives are characterized by participants clad in identical t-shirts carrying mass-distributed, commercially printed hand placards as they get off their leased school buses. Astroturf protesters demonstrate an inability to answer substantive questions regarding the topic at hand and avoid engaging with anyone they deem unsympathetic to their own views. Group members rely on directions from professional activists to prompt their actions.

Many Astroturf "protesters" are often paid from various union funds or grants from government "community outreach" programs. Volunteer activists at the neighborhood level, and their paid regional supervisors, display a marked inability to act without orders from national personages. The sites of Astroturf demonstrations are usually evident by the amount of trash left behind by those purportedly concerned about the environment and "mother earth".

However, the hallmarks of true conservative grassroots movements generally include participants who arrive from home or "well dressed" from work in their own vehicle, from which they retrieve the sign they made on the kitchen table the night before. They have educated themselves on the issue, are prepared to support their views and willing to give reasonable opposition a fair hearing. Each person attends of their own volition and with full recognition they are responsible for any speech or actions prompted by their personal motivation.

Grassroots citizen activists are volunteers, often paying out-of-pocket for expenses or raising funds from within the local group. They, more often than not, dedicate untold hours at the sacrifice of work, family and personal recreation: in essence, they invest sweat equity. Front-line organizers are nimble at overcoming obstacles, organize local activities independently, implement their own groups' tactics and strategies, and participate nationally to whatever extent they deem appropriate. The parks and other rally points for conservative protests are left cleaner than before the event. The only evidence of a large crowd is usually neatly tied trash bags gathered around public trash bins.

The heartland of America can see the plain difference. Every time the Progressives denigrate the Tea Party grassroots movement as racist or artificial Astroturf, more fed-up members of the silent majority make a sign and go to a rally.

It was the great overreach by the radical Progressives that aroused the silent majority as no other government power grab has in the history of the Republic. Citizens, who only last year still sat on their couches and yelled at the TV, became enraged by the deliberate disregard, rank hypocrisy, and arrogance displayed by Progressive elected officials.

The patriots' primary motivation was to conserve the rights and liberties guaranteed by the Constitution, and to restore a responsible representative government. There was the final realization that, in our Republic, true political power came from "we, the people", not the career politicians trying to wield authority by force of government. American citizens began exercising their sovereign power by exerting pressure on their non-representing representatives.

Chapter Four

The Politicians:
Non-Representing Representatives

"Men who look upon themselves born to reign,
and others to obey, soon grow insolent;
selected from the rest of mankind
their minds are early poisoned by importance;
and the world they act in differs so materially
from the world at large,
that they have but little opportunity of knowing its true interest,
and when they succeed to the government
are frequently the most ignorant and unfit
of any throughout the dominions."
- Thomas Paine, "Common Sense", 1776

"The Constitution begins with the words 'We, the people', not 'we the congress'," stated a woman participant at a huge Tea Party rally in Sacramento CA.[65] She expressed simply what the founders had known; that to preserve liberty the country's political power had to reside and emanate from the citizens. It is from "We, the people" that the Constitution derives its authority, for the powers conferred upon the government are only with the consent of the governed.

"The words 'people of the United States' and 'citizens' are synonymous terms," wrote Supreme Court Chief Justice Taney in 1857. "They both describe the political body who, according to our republican institutions, form the sovereignty, and

---

[65] The "Eco-Tyranny" Tea Party rally in Sacramento CA was held on August 28, 2009. Participant interview by Fox News.

who hold the power and conduct the government through their representative." Taney concluded, "They are what we familiarly call the 'sovereign people', and every citizen is one of this people, and a constituent member of this sovereignty."[66]

It was the people, and the states in which they reside, that created the federal government and charged it, in the Preamble of the Constitution, with the great responsibility to "form a more perfect union, establish justice, insure domestic tranquility, provide for the common defense, promote the general welfare, and secure the blessings of liberty to ourselves and our posterity". Although perverted over the last century by Progressives, to the founding fathers "promote the general welfare" meant government actions that benefited the whole of the country and limited to those powers specified to them in the Constitution.

"With respect to the two words 'general welfare'," wrote James Madison in a letter to James Robertson, "I have always regarded them as qualified by the detail of powers connected with them. To take them in a literal and unlimited sense would be a metamorphosis of the Constitution into a character which there is a host of proofs was not contemplated by its creators." Madison led the discussion at the Constitutional Convention in 1787, based on his extensive three-month study of republics, federations, and democracies of the past. He was the primary author of the Constitution of the United States.

To the Progressive political class the concept of "and our posterity" seems to have been forgotten entirely, as paying the bills for spending at present is put off to future generations.

---

[66] 19 Howard 393, 404 (1857).

True consideration for those not-yet-born has never been a hallmark of the Progressive Movement.

It has been the Progressive's penchant for seeing the Constitution as a "living document" that has brought us the overbearing central government under which productive Americans suffer today. As Obama stated in his 2001 public radio interview, he believes the Constitution is flawed, in that "it didn't break free from the essential constraints placed by the founding fathers".[67] If, indeed, the Constitution is a "living document" then we are no longer a nation of laws, but of the whims of man. It is the determination to restore the Constitution, and the limited government and personal liberty it guarantees, which fuels the Tea Party Movement.

Under the Constitution, congress has certain and delineated powers. The House of Representatives has the sole authority to initiate and approve, with Senate concurrence, appropriation bills and direct the spending of taxpayer dollars. Congress is solely responsible for the budget of the United States. It is the congress that writes the tax code, and congress that sets the fiscal policy of the nation. It is the congress, through the power of taxation and regulation, which exerts the current heavy burden on the liberty of the individual, a burden that would be scandalous to the authors of the Constitution.

It is our elected representatives who are responsible, because of the laws they pass, for the domestic problems facing

---

[67] WBEZ.FM Chicago Public Radio, 2001. You Tube video: http://www.youtube.com/watch?v=NTCNK7v3J6w

the nation. Yet, they continually claim their newest legislative initiatives will fix the problems they themselves created.

Unfortunately for the taxpayer, actually fixing the nations' problems is not the real mission for many of our politicians. The cunning and self-serving have a personal agenda that is consumed with amassing more power and more money, and the agenda of Progressive politicians is dedicated to limiting the individual in favor of the collective.

The list of the egregious actions of congress galvanizing the silent majority during the first months of the Tea Party movement is long. The affronts to the citizenry began with the passage of TARP in October 2008, and picked up pace with the Stimulus Bill and the controlled bankruptcies of the car companies, igniting the spot fires in February and March. The passage of Cap & Trade, by the House of Representatives, and the introduction of the health care reform bill were direct attacks on the freedom of the individual.

It was the growing understanding, on the part of citizens, about the consequences of these anti-capitalist schemes that propelled the brush fires of freedom from April on into August.

Over the past century, Progressive politicians in both major political parties have purposely designed the legislative process to be as complex and incomprehensible as possible, in order to prevent the citizenry from following the proceedings and to hide their graft and corruption. It has become a successful strategy for them.

Tea Party patriots and other like-minded folks began to realize that to truly understand the seemingly illogical policy choices and legislative actions of the current political class, it was imperative to discern the motives and philosophical intents of the Progressive Movement. Most Americans who are members of the formerly-silent majority, view proposed government action from the perspective of someone who supports and believes in free market capitalism and individual liberty. When the recent actions of elected officials are evaluated based on those values, a stark reality emerges.

The motives behind the actions of the political class appear to divide into three categories, with a fair amount of combination and migration between philosophies and intentions. About one-third of our professional politicians thirst only for their own power, one-third think we common folk are incapable of understanding complex financial and economic issues, and the final third are Progressives who work for, and are dedicated to, the downfall of capitalism and negating the freedoms guaranteed the people by our Constitution.

Many of our politicians have no understanding of, or relationship to, the Constitution or the philosophy of our founders. Their party leadership supplies the little knowledge they possess about any issue under consideration. Democrat or Republican, it doesn't matter, they are a reliable vote for whatever the party wants, unless they can cut a better deal with the other side. The prevailing wind in politics has been blowing from the radical-left for so long that an unconscionable number of our elected representatives are unaware of the true goals of Progressivism.

They are blinded by personal power, and their own egos, to the eroding effects of Progressive policies on a free people and our way of life.

These "representatives" are more than comfortable with the trappings of their very privileged life, and see no reason to stir up trouble in their "go-along to get-along" bubble. They think, "all this talk about radicals leading the country into socialism" is the result of "deliberate misinformation just meant to poison the policy debate". This pattern of thinking enables them to dismiss the reasonable concerns of their constituents. They deny that they are enabling, through their laziness and greed, the destruction of free market capitalism.

Other members of the professional political class have such a personal sense of superiority that it leads them to truly believe they "know what's best for everyone", a core Progressive mind-set. They are convinced their elite education, careers, and "experience in these matters" gives them the special insight and knowledge to make any and all decisions for the people. Because their intentions are based on "doing good" for the common man, it follows that their policies must be for the greater good as well. If their ideas fail it is obviously because the people have not recognized the genius of their policies and plans. The little people, you know, "they just don't understand".

T. S. Eliot once observed, "Half the harm that is done in this world is due to people who want to feel important. They don't mean to do harm, but the harm does not interest them. Or they do not see it, or they justify it, because they are absorbed in the endless struggle to think well of themselves."

The bitterest pill is the realization that there are really politicians and political operatives, people who have benefited mightily from the abundance and freedoms of America, who work to eradicate the spirit of individual liberty and personal responsibility. These avowed Progressives are dedicated to tearing down America's traditions and values.

For the last one hundred years the political ranks have been saturated with Progressives who deliberately accept, believe, and actively participate in the implementation of Marxist-based programs designed to bankrupt America and implement a collective society. The goals, strategies and tactics of modern Progressives are outlined in the Cloward-Piven Strategy. Andrew Cloward and Frances Fox Piven, a married couple, were self-declared communists and sociology professors teaching at Columbia University when they developed their strategy to destroy the American free market system in the mid-1960's. Their strategy was drawn from the writings and philosophy of Saul Alinsky, the infamous Marxist community organizer working in Chicago from the 1930's through the early 1960's. Cloward-Piven tactics are designed to bring about the fall of capitalism by overloading and undermining government bureaucracy with ever-increasing demands for goods and services for the "poor and disenfranchised".

These political goals include government control of private industries, unsustainable spending on wealth redistribution programs, and breaking the capitalist free market economic engine through the restriction of energy.

They have divided the people by using hyphens to modify their identification as Americans (African-American, Mexican-American, etc.), making their "Americanism" a second-tier partner in a dual-identity citizen.

The only logical explanation for such destructive actions is that these politicians are at the specific service of the ultimate Progressive goal: the destruction of free market capitalism and individual liberty in America, and replacing our Constitutional Republic with a socialist-collective society with themselves in positions of total power.

The number of elected officials who truly understand the Constitution, and the limited government designed to protect and promote individual liberty, are sadly few in number. They fight valiantly against the Progressive tide and are regularly derided in the establishment media and academic circles as "mean spirited".

When the newly aware citizens compared and contrasted the unfolding events against the liberty-based philosophical underpinnings that our founders had included in the Constitution, they found these Progressive-based policies, programs, and plans, to be clear and present dangers to the Republic. Learning to recognize the goal of Progressive policies to undermine American individualism, its double-speak and tactics, is key to understanding the complex tangle of these overwhelmingly huge and massive bills. The strongest defense against tyranny is an educated citizenry.

TARP: TROUBLED ASSET RELIEF PROGRAM

In September 2008, the Bush Administration pushed for adoption of the three-page "Paulson Plan", named after the Secretary of the Treasury, which began the autumn spending orgy known as TARP.

Secretary Paulson stated during his testimony before the Senate, "We must avoid a continuing series of financial institution failures and frozen credit markets that threaten American families' financial well-being, the viability of businesses both small and large, and the very health of our economy." He concluded, "This troubled asset purchase program on its own is the single most effective thing we can do to help homeowners, the American people and stimulate our economy."

Representative Spencer Bachus (R-AL) called the must-pass-now proposal and the attendant threat of a massive economic collapse, "a gun to our head."[68] (One year later, on October 5, 2009, the Inspector General for TARP, Neil Barofsky, announced that Secretary Paulson and the Chairman of the Federal Reserve Bank, Ben Bernanke, misled the American people when they stated the first nine banks to receive $125 billion in TARP funds were sound, when they were not.[69])

The TARP proposal grew to over 100 pages after committee mark-up, and was brought before the full House on September 29, 2008 as an amendment to unrelated legislation. Reacting to the massive opposition expressed by their constituents,

---

[68] CBS News November 12, 2008:
http://www.cbsnews.com/stories/2008/11/12/politics/main4595351.shtml
[69] Fox News, October 5, 2009:
http://www.foxnews.com/politics/2009/10/05/government-report-questions-bank-rescue-claims/

the House rejected the amendment by voting 228 to 205. It appeared that the overwhelming opposition by concerned American citizens had prevailed.

However, the Senate was considering their version of the defeated House amendment. Despite Constitutional provisions making the House the originator of spending bills, the Senate substituted their 451-page version of TARP as an amendment to a previously passed House bill. On October 1, 2008 the Senate voted 74-25 to pass the Troubled Asset Relief Program.

The amended version was then sent to the House of Representatives for consideration. On October 3, 2008 the House voted to enact the program with a vote of 263-171. President Bush signed the law within hours of its passage. TARP increased the 2008 federal budget by 24% from $2.9 trillion to a total of $3.6 trillion, exceeding the congressionally approved ceiling of $3.1 trillion. The total government commitment and proposed commitments for bailouts, including interest, is reportedly $1 trillion. The whole economy of the United States is estimated to be $14 trillion.[70]

It did not take a Harvard degree for the average American to understand that this money would have to be repaid, and it would be repaid from his pocket and the pockets of his children. The majority response of the country to congress was an overwhelming "No!", but the message went unheard or unheeded. As Senator Dianne Feinstein (D-CA) so famously said, "I've received 91,000 phone calls and emails from California, 85,000 of them opposed to this measure."

[70] CBS News November 12, 2008:
http://www.cbsnews.com/stories/2008/11/12/politics/main4595351.shtml

When Senator Feinstein voted "yes" she belittled the will of her constituents.

The impending collapse of the financial institutions was the direct result of federal regulations contained in the Community Reinvestment Act (CRA). The CRA was originally passed during the Carter Administration with the supposed purpose to limit the practice by lending institutions of refusing home mortgages in specific low income urban areas, generally known as "red-lining". The original CRA only mandated that banks make sound loans in these areas, and this standard prevailed until the Clinton Administration.

During the 1990's the CRA was amended, almost on a yearly basis, to require 30% of loans be made in low-income areas in order for banks to be judged in compliance. In 2000, the federally backed institutions of Fannie Mae and Freddie Mac were required to have 50% of their business in CRA loans, a $500 billion investment.

By 2005, private lending institutions had also reached a 50% level of CRA loans in their portfolios. In order not to run afoul of federal regulators, these loans, more often than not, were made with no down payment and no proof of income required of the loan applicant. The responsibility for banks making "risky" loans lies squarely at the feet of congress.

In addition to covering the worthless mortgage derivatives, TARP funds were also used to bail out corporate giants like Goldman Sachs and American International Group (AIG). Goldman Sachs led in the bundling of the CRA mortgages into derivative securities.

AIG provided the insurance guarantees behind the mortgage derivatives, and used TARP funds to pay their obligations to their European bank clients. AIG also underwrites the health care and pension benefits enjoyed by members of congress.

Citizen patriot, Ken Russell of Alton IL, expressed the concerns of many of his fellow Americans. "I would like to know exactly what happened in the meeting with Paulson, Bernanke and congress and why an entire collapse of the economy would or could occur without it [TARP]." Russell continued, "I believe that allowing irresponsible banks to fail would have been best. Get the deserved pain over now instead of holding it off and making the inevitable worse. President Bush's remark 'We have to suspend free market capitalism in order to save it' was the dumbest statement of all time behind Vice President Biden's, 'You have to go into debt in order to get out of bankruptcy.'"

Russell concluded, "No country has ever been more vulnerable to economic collapse in world history than the United States. And our response is a never-ending effort to spend more money we do not have. It is stunning."

AUTO COMPANY BAILOUTS

During the last months of 2008, the federal government bailed out General Motors and Chrysler with TARP funds, which went beyond the original scope of the legislation, in order to protect union health and retirement benefits. Within weeks of the November election, House Speaker Nancy Pelosi (D-CA) was confident that the congress would find "emergency and limited financial assistance" for the auto industry in the recently passed

$800 billion TARP. Pelosi also stated that any assistance to the industry would include limits on executive pay, "rigorous" government review authority, and taxpayer protections.

Senator Jeff Sessions (R-AL) voiced the growing skepticism, "Once we cross the divide from financial institutions to individual corporations, truly, where would you draw the line?"[71] But as Ken Russell, citizen and patriot, asked, "Why isn't a government take-over of banks also crossing the line? Hmmmm?"

In early December 2008 a CNN/Opinion Research Corp survey showed 61% of Americans "dead set" against the federal bail out of the auto giants, with only 36% favoring. The party affiliation breakdown showed 70% of Republicans opposed the auto bailout, 62% of Independents, and 55% of registered Democrats.[72]

The stated purpose of the auto bailout was to prevent the companies from going into bankruptcy. However, Nobel Prize-winning economist Gary Becker rightly pointed out that bankruptcy court was precisely the appropriate antidote. "The main problem with American auto companies," he explained, "is that during the good times of the 1970's, 1980's and 1990's, they made overly generous settlements with the United Auto Workers (UAW) on wages, pensions, and health benefits." Becker continued, "In those days, the UAW was one of the most powerful unions in the U.S., and it bargained aggressively with the auto manufacturers, carrying out strikes when its demands were not met."

---

[71] CBS News November 12, 2008:
http://www.cbsnews.com/stories/2008/11/12/politics/main4595351.shtml
[72] CNN December 3, 2008:
http://cnn.site.printthis.clickability.com/pt/cpt?action=cpt&title=Six+in+10+oppose+auto+baillut%2C+pol

Becker pointed to the thriving American plants of Japanese and German auto manufacturers that set up in southern and border-states where they could avoid the UAW and utilize efficient methods of production. About one-third of all cars produced in the United States come from foreign owned plants. Becker wrote, "Bankruptcy would help GM become more competitive by abrogating significant parts of their labor contracts with the UAW".

Becker concluded, "Is GM 'too big' to fail? I do not believe the company is too big to go into a reorganization – which is what bankruptcy would involve. Such reorganization would abrogate its untenable labor contracts, and give it a chance to survive in the long run. A bail out, by contrast, would simply postpone the needed reforms in these labor contracts, the business model of GM, and its management."[73]

In December 2008 congress approved $17 billion in federal funds to help GM and Chrysler "survive", and demanded that both companies submit restructuring plans. By accepting federal funding, the automakers placed their private corporate decisions under the control of congress and the president.

---

[73] Gary Becker: http://www.becker-posner-blog.com/archieves/2008/11/bail_out_the_bi.html

STIMULUS BILL:
AMERICAN RECOVERY AND REINVESTMENT ACT

In early 2009, with a deep recession facing the country, the Progressive Democrat controlled congress abandoned all known successful economic strategies used in a capitalist system for recovery: tax cuts, investment incentives, and easing restrictive regulations. Instead, they burdened the money supply by borrowing huge sums to fund public projects in favored congressional districts, and to give grants to local and state governments to protect public-sector jobs. This resulted in restricting the credit for small business owners and entrepreneurs. Congress then added insult to injury by proposing tax increases for the enterprises that account for 90% of American jobs.

Within the first three weeks of President Obama's administration, congress passed the Stimulus Bill (American Recovery and Reinvestment Act). The original House version of the bill carried a price tag of $787 billion, with another $100 billion added by the Senate.

Real job-creating infrastructure projects accounted for only 10% of the funding.[74] The bill was really a Christmas tree of gifts to the Progressive left. The Act included expansion of social welfare provisions, funding for "green" energy, and health care studies on the effectiveness of medical treatments, which would be an integral part of the proposed health care plan. ($1.1 billion was appropriated for the formation of the "Federal Coordinating Council for Comparative Effectiveness Research". Comparative

---

[74] Details of the awards to the various Congressional Districts can be viewed at www.recovery.gov.

119

effectiveness research provides information on the relative strengths and weakness of various medical interventions.)

Representative Dave Obey (D-WI) introduced the Stimulus Bill on January 26, 2009, and it buzzed through both the House Committee on Appropriations and the House Committee on the Budget. Two days later, on January 28th, the bill passed the full House with votes only from the Democrat majority. Eleven Democrats, so-called "blue dogs" (Democrats from conservative districts), crossed the aisle to vote against the bill with all 177 Republicans. Within two weeks it passed the Senate on February 10th, with the joint conference committee reporting out a final bill in just two days.

In the new era of "cooperation" promised by President Obama and House Speaker Pelosi, the rules of engagement for Republicans became "join the Democrats or be ignored". On February 12th, Minority Leader John Boehner (R-OH) confirmed that the House Republican leadership had been kept out of the House-Senate conference that was responsible for the final version of the bill.

House Speaker Pelosi commenting on the criticism of the conference committee said, "Not only just I had to see it, I had to show it to my colleagues and my caucus. We wanted to take all the time that was necessary to make sure it was right." Apparently, two days is enough time to thoughtfully consider spending $800 billion that doesn't exist.

Stung by being caught up short on their promises, Majority Leader Steny Hoyer (D-MD), responded, "The conference report text will be filed this evening, giving members enough time to review the conference report before voting on it tomorrow afternoon." The final text became available late that night at 11:00 p.m., approximately 10 hours before Friday's session, and 38 hours less than the promised "public transparency".

Twitter was the medium of choice for some congressional members to urge action by their colleagues. Senator Claire McCaskill (D-MO) twittered, "Don't know when we're going to vote. Will the no votes delay vote just because they can? Speed is important. They know that." A swift reply came from House Republican Whip Eric Cantor (R-VA), "Those in favor of speed over commonsense may just be afraid of letting the People know what they are ramming through."

On Friday, February 13th the bill passed the House of Representatives on a straight party line (excepting six Blue Dogs) vote of 246-183, and in the Senate by 60-38 with three Republicans joining the Democrat pork feeding-frenzy. President Obama signed the Stimulus Bill into law on February 17, 2009.

Not only did the politicians not read the Stimulus Bill before voting, there is credible evidence they didn't even write significant portions of it. One component of the Stimulus Bill was major investment in the development of "clean energy". On the same day President Obama signed the bill, Senator Harry Reid released a statement acknowledging the role played by the Apollo Alliance in writing the bill.

The Apollo Alliance, a Progressive organization, was formed in 2003 to partner the environmental movement with sections of the business community. Jeff Jones, co-founder with Bill Ayers of the 1960's radical group Weather Underground (known for bombing police stations and the Pentagon), is the Chairman of the New York Apollo Alliance. Major funding for the Apollo Alliance comes from the Tides Foundation and multi-billionaire George Soros.

Reid stated, "This legislation is the first step in building a clean energy economy that creates jobs and moves us closer to solving our enormous energy and environmental challenges." He continued, "We've talked about moving forward on these ideas for decades. The Apollo Alliance has been an important factor in helping us develop and execute a strategy that makes great progress on these goals and in motivating the public to support them."[75]

In September 2008 the Apollo Alliance had published _The New Apollo Program_, calling for a comprehensive investment strategy and implementation plan by the federal government costing $500 billion over 10 years. The Stimulus Bill that they "helped" to write would ensure that government support.

It was during these same beginning weeks of the Obama Administration that the first tax revolt protests began to appear. Two days after Obama signed the "Porkulus Package" came Rick Santelli's clarion call and the resulting response from the over-taxed and ignored electorate. A common sentiment shared by many people was disgust with their so-called representatives that not only did they not read the bill, they didn't even write it, before voting for passage.

---

[75] Apollo Alliance website "At Last Federal Government Signs Up for Clean Energy Economy by Keith Schneider, February 17, 2009: http://apolloalliance.org/feature-articles/at-last-federal-government-signs-up-for-clean-energy-economy/

Jeff Jarvis, a Tea Party Patriot from Ohio, noted, "The congressional system is designed to allow for slow, careful deliberation. This process was thwarted by the false imperative presented by the Democrat supporters of the bill." Charlie Johnson, a concerned citizen in Little Rock AR, opined, "The Stimulus Bill was a payoff to insiders and big banks. As time went along we found the big banks only invested the money to enrich themselves and as some suspected would happen, Wall Street prospered while Main Street boarded up many windows and went home."

CONTROLLED BANKRUPTCIES AND
AUTO COMPANY TAKE-OVERS

Soon the executive branch moved outside of traditional regulatory roles and began dictating operating decisions in privately held companies. President Obama appointed Stephen Ratner as "car czar". Ratner was one of 32 special advisors to the president that became known to the public as "czars". Most of these advisors were not subject to congressional approval or oversight, answering only to the president.

In reports filed with the government in February 2009, General Motors requested another $16.6 billion. GM owed roughly $28 billion to bondholders (first line secured debt), and another $20 billion to its union-operated retiree health care trust (second tier unsecured debt).

In late March 2009, President Obama refused more long-term federal bailouts for General Motors and Chrysler, and raised the possibility of a "controlled bankruptcy" for one or both of them.

In an ironic effort to reassure consumers, Obama announced the federal government would back the warranties that new car buyers receive. In a statement read at the White House, Obama stated he was "absolutely committed" to the survival of the automakers, but "our auto industry is not moving in the right direction fast enough."

The "right direction", according to the Progressive agenda, would be for the auto industry to focus on the supposed public benefits that would accrue from building electric and hybrid cars. In reality, the Progressive agenda was to create an auto industry that was comprised of "permanently government-subsidized and government-run organizations that employ an inefficient and unmotivated workforce to produce small, underpowered cars at a financial loss," as explained by market analyst Robert Tracinski.[76]

For the first time in our country's history, a sitting president fired the Chief Executive Officer of a private company. On March 29th the Obama Administration forced the ouster of Rick Wagoner from his post as CEO of General Motors, and implied the same executive control over Chrysler. The forced retirement of Wagoner on that Sunday paved the way for Obama's remarks the following day. "This is not meant as a criticism of Mr. Wagoner, who has devoted his life to this company, rather it's a recognition that it will take a new vision

---

[76] Real Clear Markets November 18, 2008, "Auto Bailouts Will Give Us Detroitsky" by Robert Tracinski:
http://www.realclermarkets.com/articles/2008/11/auto_bailouts_will_give_us _det.html

and new direction to create the GM of the future."[77] Apparently Obama believes it is in his power as president to dictate the vision and future direction of private sector business.

Other changes at GM included new directors on its board. Fritz Henderson, GM's president and chief operating officer, became the new CEO. Mr. Henderson later resigned from this post on December 1, 2009. Board member Kent Kresa, former chairman and CEO of defense contractor Northrop Grumman Corp, issued a written statement, "The board has recognized for some time that the company's restructuring will likely cause a significant change in the stockholders of the company and create the need for new directors with additional skills and experience."

The "significant change in the stockholders" would be in reference to the pending new ownership stake to be controlled by the United Auto Workers (UAW). Therefore, the need for "new directors with additional skills and experience" would open the door for union bosses to take their seats at the board table, an obvious payback for UAW support for Democrat candidates and causes over the last several decades.

At the same moment in which the president was dictating who would be at the helm of General Motors, Obama stated, "Let me be clear, the United States government has no interest in running GM. We have no intention in running GM." For someone not interested in running car companies, it appeared that Obama was doing that exact thing.

---

[77] My Central Jersey March 30, 2009, "Obama Refuses More Bailouts for Auto Industry" by Philip Elliott:
http://www.mycentraljersey.com/apps/pbcs.dll/article?AID=/20090330/NATIONALWORLD/

The Chrysler Corporation entered bankruptcy on April 30th with a government-approved plan to be bought out by the Italian automaker, Fiat. The most troubling aspect of the "controlled bankruptcy" was the overturning of over 200 years of law and precedent. Bankruptcies are by nature a dividing up of the leftover assets among creditors, and not all creditors are equal. It has long been established law that first line, or secured, investors lend money at a lower rate in exchange for more protection in the bankruptcy process. These claims rank above others, including shareholders and employees.

The government-backed "controlled bankruptcy" turned this body of laws on its head. The bankruptcy court negated the traditional "first in line" protected position of the secured creditors in favor of the UAW contract-mandated claims. Most of the secured creditors were investments in the individual retirement accounts held by many American citizens. The court ordered their recovery to be only 28 cents per dollar of their $7 billion investment; while the UAW would receive 43 cents per dollar on its $11 billion claim, and a majority stake in the restructured firm.[78]

The bankruptcy court nullified first-line creditors and their legitimate claims. President Obama denounced those private investors who objected as "speculators". Yet it was the government that actually committed unlawful actions by putting the UAW claims above lawful secured creditors. When Chrysler emerged from bankruptcy on June 11th, the U.S. government owned 10% of the company.

---

[78] The Economist Newspaper and The Economist Group "Barack Obama and the Carmakers, An Offer You Can't Refuse", May 7, 2009: http://www.economist.com/PrinterFriendly.cfm?story_id-13610871

The Economist newspaper's web site asked, "If bankruptcy becomes a tool of social policy, who will then lend to struggling firms in which the government has a political interest?"

In the midst of the Chrysler bankruptcy, General Motors filed court papers on June 1st and entered into the same "controlled" process. Once again, first line creditors were denied their traditional bankruptcy status in favor of the UAW.

When the "General Motors Company" emerged from bankruptcy, its ownership consisted of the U.S. government with 61%, the UAW with 17.5%, the Canadian government with 11.5%, and the remaining 10% controlled by unsecured bondholders.[79]

In June 2009, the Congressional Budget Office estimated that taxpayers would lose about $40 billion of the first $55 billion in aid. In total the U.S. government provided the auto industry with $81 billion. The Congressional Oversight Panel for TARP released a report on September 9th, estimating that most of the $23 billion initially provided the automakers would probably not be repaid. The prospect of the U.S. taxpayer ever recovering funds from the government's assistance to the auto industry would depend on the stock in the companies rising to levels above those they held before bankruptcy. The panel's report stated this was "highly unlikely". The report also recommended that the Treasury Department should consider placing the auto company holdings into an independent trust to avoid any "conflict of interest".[80]

---

[79] Manufacturing.net website "GM, Chrysler Bankruptcy Cases At A Glance", July 6, 2009: http://www.manufacturing.net/News-GM-Chrysler-Bankruptcy-Cases-At-A-Glance-070609.aspx

[80] Fox News website "Taxpayers Face Heavy Losses on Auto Bailout", by the Associated Press, September 9, 2009:

The original rationale of the federal taxpayer aid was to prevent GM and Chrysler from going into bankruptcy. However they still ended up in court, but instead of the traditional free market bankruptcy solution they became wards of the state. The UAW remained intact and part owner of the companies at the expense of secured bondholders. It is not unreasonable to think that the end result was the Progressive's plan from the start.

Jeff Jarvis, a patriot in Ohio, stated, "I was not really surprised by the auto bankruptcies. I knew that contracts between the automakers and unions have been detrimental to the automakers existence, but I didn't realize how much. The front office shares much of the blame." Ken Russell, of Illinois, was also not surprised by the final outcome, "The auto bail out was not about cars. It was about preserving union pension funds and paying them back for their votes and political support. Robbing the board of director seats on GM and Chrysler, so the congress and the unions could hold the majority vote, was also unconstitutional."

CAP AND TRADE:
CONTROLLING AMERICA'S ENERGY

Controlling and eliminating the traditional American sources of energy has long been a goal of the Progressive left. Our abundant resources of coal, oil, and natural gas provide 85% of America's energy.

---

http://www.foxnews.com/politics/elections/2009/09/09/taxpayers-face-heavy-losses-auto-bailout/

Their plan has been to use the environmental canard of man-made global warming to hobble the great engine of the American economy, and their vehicle is a scheme known as "Cap and Trade".

Despite the declarations of former Vice-President Al Gore, the science of man-made global warming is far from settled. Over 31,000 American scientists have signed a petition publicly repudiating the Kyoto Accord, which declared man-made global warming the greatest threat to mankind and imposed a Cap and Trade system on signatories.[81]

However, it is established science that the earth, throughout its history, has been through many cycles of global warming and cooling, some quite pronounced, as a natural result of being part of a dynamic solar system. Higher levels of carbon dioxide (CO^2) in the atmosphere follow periods of warming, not precede them as claimed by the man-made global warming hoaxers. Historically, mankind and civilization fare far better in times of climate warming than when conditions are cooler, such as during the Roman and Medieval warm periods. These historic pre-industrial warm periods are curiously absent from the "studies" submitted by the "scientist" proponents of man-made global warming.

Water vapor composes ninety-five percent of greenhouse gases. Of the remaining 5%, carbon dioxide accounts for less than one percent. Far from being a pollutant, carbon dioxide is a part of the cycle of life. All living beings, including humans, exhale

---

[81] Global Warming Petition Project has signatures from 31,478 American scientists, including 9,029 with Ph.D.'s: http://www.petitionproject.org

carbon dioxide with every breath. Crops, grasses, bushes, and trees then take in the carbon dioxide from the air and through photosynthesis they produce the oxygen needed by living beings to breathe. That is why burning wood, coal or oil releases carbon dioxide. It is held within these natural earth substances. All life on earth is carbon based, therefore attempts to control carbon are attempts to control all aspects of life on earth.

The Cap and Trade scheme would put a limit on the amount of carbon dioxide an energy company or manufacturer can emit. Firms would be required to have a permit for specific amounts of emissions they would be allowed. The permits would have an enforceable limit, or "cap".

Some companies would find it easier to meet their cap than others, and they could then sell or "trade" their permits to those with higher operating emissions. This is the rationale for achieving a supposed nationwide reduction in emissions. Over time the limits will become stricter, until companies are competing to achieve lower and lower energy emission levels than are produced today, effectively limiting the production of energy and manufacturing output.

The Chicago Climate Exchange (CCX) was formed in 2003 to provide the trading structure for carbon credits. An early major investor in CCX was the Joyce Foundation, with an initial investment of $1.1 million. Members of the Board of Directors when this investment was made were Barack Obama and Valerie Jarrett, long-time Obama friend and now a White House Advisor. The 5th largest investor in CCX was the London-based company "generation", co-founded by Al Gore. In 2006, Goldman Sachs, an eventual recipient of bailout funds, purchased 10% of CCX. One day after the 2006

130

election, after the Democrat Party secured control of congress, Franklin Raines (former head of the Office of Management and Budget in the Clinton Administration), bought the patent for a process designed to facilitate carbon trading, under his authority as head of Fannie Mae.[82] Why would the government-run home mortgage corporations want or need to control the mechanism for carbon credit exchange?

The stated goal of Cap and Trade according to John Podesta, former chief-of-staff for President Clinton, and now President and CEO of the Center for American Progress is, "to limit the rise in global temperature to approximately 2.0 degrees Celsius (3.6 degrees Fahrenheit) above pre-industrial levels by 2050, by reducing carbon dioxide and other emissions from companies as part of a larger plan for curbing global warming."[83] In an interview with the *San Francisco Chronicle* on January 17, 2008, then presidential candidate Obama stated, "What I've said is that we would put a Cap and Trade system in place that is as aggressive, if not more aggressive, than anybody else's out there."

Obama continued in detail, "I was the first to call for a 100% auction on the Cap and Trade system, which means that every unit of carbon or greenhouse gases emitted would be charged to the polluter. That will create a market in which whatever technologies are out there, that are being presented, whatever power plants that are being built, that they would have to meet the rigors of that market and the ratcheted down caps that are being placed, imposed every year."

---

[82] Fox News, *"Glenn Beck Show"*, April 26 and 29, 2010. During his 5 years as head of Fannie Mae, Franklin Raines received $90 million in bonuses.
[83] Center for American Progress website, "Cap and Trade 101" by John Podesta, January 16, 2008:
www.americanprogress.org/issues/2008/01/capandtrade101.html

"So if somebody wants to build a coal-powered plant, they can," he reasoned, "it's just that it will bankrupt them because they're going to be charged a huge sum for all that greenhouse gas that's being emitted."[84] Obama concluded, "Under my plan of a Cap and Trade system, electricity rates will necessarily skyrocket."[85]

According to research done by the Heritage Foundation, "while the costs of aggressive Cap and Trade proposals are substantial, the environmental benefits are suspect. This is true even if one fully accepts the claim of man-made global warming." The report continues, "The most ambitious measure to date is the Kyoto Protocol, but even if the U.S. were a party to this treaty and the European nations and other signatories were in full compliance (most are unlikely to meet their targets), the treaty would reduce the Earth's future temperature by an estimate 0.07 degrees Celsius by 2050 – an amount too small to even verify."

The report concluded, "Cap and Trade bills are nothing short of a government re-engineering of the American economy. With its aggressive targets to reduce emissions from fossil fuels use, it would put the nation on a path of serious economic harm not justified by any benefits."[86]

On May 15, 2009 Henry Waxman (D-CA) and Edward Markey (D-MA), introduced the American Clean Energy and

---

[84] You Tube video: http://www.youtube.com/watch?v=Hdi4onAQBWQ
[85] Washington Examiner "Obama's Plan 'Necessarily' Skyrockets Energy Bills" by Paul Chesser, May 1, 2009: http://www.washingtonexaminer.com/opinion/OpEd-Contributor/Obamas-plan-necessarily-skyrockets-energy-bills-44124402.html
[86] Heritage Foundation website, "Beware of Cap and Trade Climate Bills" by Ben Lieberman, December 6, 2007: www.heritage.org/Research/Economy/wm1723.cfm

Security Act, also known as Cap and Trade, to the House of Representatives. The 1,427-page bill would restrict greenhouse gas emissions from industries that burn coal, oil, and natural gas. Electricity producers, oil refineries, and natural gas companies would be required to obtain permits for each ton of carbon dioxide they produce. The cost of the permits is essentially a tax. As the government will issue fewer allowances in each following year, the cost of the permits will rise every year. As with any tax, the cost will be passed on to consumers for the energy they personally use and in the products they purchase.

The real carrot behind the stick is more tax revenue for the federal government. According to Podesta, "Initial estimates by the Congressional Budget Office project that an economy-wide Cap and Trade program would generate at least $50 billion per year, but could reach up to $300 billion."[87] The starting point for Cap and Trade programs has the government selling 100% of the cap permits.

However, this amount of money has attracted a steady stream of lobbyists seeking a share for their clients. The Center for Public Integrity estimates that over 2,300 lobbyists were involved with the Cap and Trade legislation. Congress was more than willing to listen to all comers. For the first 15 years of Cap and Trade over 88% of government revenue from the emission permits is to be given to various special interest groups.

---

[87] Center for American Progress website, "Cap and Trade 101" by John Podesta, January 16, 2008:
www.americanprogress.org/issues/2008/01/capandtrade101.html

According to the Heritage Foundation research, "The total value of the allowances (the tax revenue) would be hundreds of billions of dollars per year and will have an aggregate value of $5.7 trillion by 2035. This makes Waxman-Markey (Cap and Trade) one of the largest new taxes in history, if not the largest."[88]

The report lists the economic impacts on the average American family by 2035: gasoline prices will rise by 58%, natural gas by 55%, heating oil by 56%, and electricity by 90%. For a family of four, their energy costs will rise by $1,241 per year, and including taxes that cost will be $4,609. Other impacts include: falling income and savings that will result in a family of four reducing its consumption of goods and services by up to $3,000 per year, the loss of nearly 2.5 million jobs, and economic losses of $9.4 trillion. The national debt, per person, will include an additional $12,803.

Even an administration official had to admit the folly of trying to affect the world's long-term climate. In testimony before the Senate Committee on Environment and Public Works on July 7th, Environmental Protection Agency Administrator Lisa Jackson stated, "I believe the central parts of the EPA chart are that U.S. action alone will not impact world CO^2 levels."

Although President Obama and the Democrats in congress claim that Cap and Trade is a jobs bill, due to lavish subsidies for "green" jobs building solar panels and windmills, the number of these jobs will be insignificant compared to the jobs lost because of higher energy prices impacting economic growth.

---

[88] Heritage Foundation website, "Heritage Analysis of Waxman-Markey Hits Where Others Miss" by David W. Kreutzer, Ph.D., August 6, 2009: www.heritage.org/Research/EnergyandEnvironment/wm2580.cfm

(Spain implemented an aggressive "green economy" plan and lost two jobs for every one created by alternative energy technologies. That country's government is now scaling back on their original policies.)

The Heritage Foundation reports, "Green projects do not pay for themselves; it is the taxpayers who fund the research and development of renewable energy and the cost of the subsidies that are required to make renewables competitive. Yet renewable energy still only provides a small fraction of America's energy needs, and it is more expensive per kilowatt hour than traditional, reliable sources of energy." The report continued, "Consumers lose doubly, paying more as taxpayers and as ratepayers."[89]

The Heritage Foundation report concluded, "It is important to remember that everything policymakers have promised this bill will do will in fact do the opposite. Cap and Trade will drive up energy costs for years to come, resulting in economic pain and higher unemployment."

After its May 15, 2009 introduction, the Cap and Trade Bill was referred to the House Energy and Commerce Committee chaired by Representative Henry Waxman. The bill was also referred to eight other House committees.[90]

During debate in the Energy and Commerce Committee on May 20th, Republican representative Joe Barton of Texas asked Chairman Waxman if he had read the bill.

---

[89] Heritage Foundation website, "Cap and Trade Sold under False Pretenses" by Nicolas Loris and Ben Lieberman, July 8, 2009: www.heritage.org/Research/EnergyandEnvironment/wm2528.cfm

[90] Foreign Affairs, Financial Services, Education and Labor, Science and Technology, Transportation and Infrastructure, Natural Resources, Agriculture, and Ways and Means.

Waxman responded, "You asking me? I certainly don't claim to know everything that's in this bill. I know that we left it to, uh, uh, we, we relied very heavily on the scientists, on the IPCC[91] and others and the consensus that they have that there is a problem of, uh, uh, global warming." (Several important aspects of the IPCC report were discredited in late 2009 with the release of internal e-mails wherein scientists at the East Anglia University in England admitted they manipulated data to support their pre-determined conclusions. For example, temperature recording device data, tree growth ring data, and the rate of melt for Himalayan glaciers.)

Waxman continued, "It's having an impact, and that, uh, we need to try to reduce it by the amounts that they think we need to achieve in order to avoid, uh, some of the consequences." He concluded, "That's what I know, but I don't know the details."[92]

Orally reading bills in committee is a detail that is generally suspended, especially for huge Progressive legislation. However, due to the criticism from Representative Barton, Chairman Waxman announced the reading of the bill. In absolute arrogance, Waxman brought in a speed-reader to do the honors for this massive legislation. After a few minutes of this insult Barton relented and the speed-reader was relieved of his duties. By the end of the May 20th committee meeting all twenty-four amendments

---

[91] Intergovernmental Panel on Climate Change established by the United Nations Environment Programme.

[92] Video posted on Michelle Malkin website, May 21, 2009: http://michellemalkin.com/2009/05/21/waxman-clueless-about-his-captrade-bill-youre-asking-me/
Transcript posted on Rush Limbaugh website, May 29, 2009: http://www.rushlimbaugh.com/home/daily/site_052909/content/01125110.guest.html

proposed by Democrat lawmakers were approved. Only two of the seventeen amendments put forward by Republicans were accepted.

Within only six weeks of its introduction, Cap and Trade was brought to the floor of the House of Representatives for a vote on June 26, 2009. This was the last session day before congress' Fourth of July recess. That morning, at 3:47 a.m., the Rules Committee added a 310-page amendment.[93] Later that day, House Minority Leader John Boehner spoke of the problematic parts of the bill, including the last minute amendments, but was only able to delay voting for one hour.

The bill passed the House by the close vote of 219-212. The aye votes came from 211 Democrats and 8 Republicans; the noes came from 168 Republicans and 44 Democrats. Representative Patrick Kennedy (D-RI) was brought in from drug and alcohol rehab to cast his yes vote. Representative Ellen Tauscher (D-CA) delayed resigning from the House in order to preside as Speaker Pro Tempore and to vote aye. (The day before the U.S. Senate had confirmed Tauscher as the Undersecretary of State for Arms Control and International Security.) The bill was then forwarded to the Senate for consideration in the fall.

Once again massive legislation, having far reaching effects on every citizen and the economy, was rushed through and passed without most of the lawmakers bothering to know the contents and their repercussions. After their exhausting work ramming legislation through that went against the will of the American public, congress recessed for their Fourth of July vacations.

---

[93] HJ 587

Ken Russell, an Ohio citizen, stated, "Cap and Trade is nothing more than Progressive socialism-controlling behavior over what is now known to be a hoax. Have you heard anyone in congress demanding real scientists with real data be allowed to show that man-made global warming is the biggest hoax perpetrated on civilization since, well civilization started?" Gail Lightfoot, a patriot in California, affirmed, "We cannot control the globe. We may need to adapt but it is arrogant to think we can control the globe. This is a time when the market really is the best solution. Government edicts will not change the weather. Ever."

GOVERNMENT CONTROLLED HEALTH CARE

Perhaps the most contentious legislation introduced during the first six months of the Obama Administration was the health care reform bill, America's Affordable Health Choices Act. The 1,107-page HR 3200 was introduced on July 14, 2009 and sponsored by seven Democrat Representatives: John Dingall (MI), Charles Rangel (NY), Henry Waxman (CA), George Miller (CA), Pete Stark (CA), Frank Pallone (NJ), and Robert Andrews (NJ). (The bill was ultimately combined with others and became HR 3962, running over 1,900 pages by October 2009.)

The reported purpose of the bill was to provide health insurance for an estimated 30 million Americans without coverage. This figure includes those temporarily between employment, college students and young adults who do not feel the need for insurance, those that can afford insurance but choose not to purchase it, illegal aliens, and those with pre-existing conditions unable to secure health care on the open market. (Citizens with pre-

138

existing conditions are generally eligible for pool insurance guaranteed by the various state governments.) These groups account for approximately 9% of the population of the United States, yet they were given as the reason that a complete overhaul by the government of the American medical system was necessary.

The bill would impose massive changes and burdensome regulations on the delivery of health care in the United States that could eventually lead to the collapse of private insurance. During the summer of 2009, public opinion polls showed that 91% of Americans had health care insurance with 84% rating satisfaction with their plan as good or excellent.[94] Americans are the beneficiaries of the greatest health care system ever known by mankind. Under current U.S. law no one can be denied health care in a hospital, for any reason, even for the inability to pay or based on their citizenship status.

The United States leads the world with its incredible advances of modern medical technology. These advances are possible because of our free market capitalist system and the profits it affords to risk takers. Without the promise of just compensation, individuals are not motivated to invest, invent or innovate new methods and technologies.

Government-run health care always increases costs and reduces services. Canada and England have had this experience. In these countries citizens who think they are beneficiaries of government benefits find themselves really the victims of government, as regulations, in effect, cause the rationing of care under the total control of unaccountable bureaucrats.

---

[94] Fox News poll released August 13, 2009.

At the AFL-CIO Conference on Civil, Human and Women Rights in 2003, then Illinois State Senator Barack Obama stated, "I happen to be a proponent of a single-payer universal health care program." He continued, "I see no reason why the United States of America, the wealthiest country in the history of the world, spending 14% of its Gross National Product on health care cannot provide basic health insurance to everybody. A single-payer health care plan, a universal health care plan, and that's what I'd like to see."

Obama concluded with the Progressives' dream of total political control, "But as all of you know, we may not get there immediately. Because first we have to take back the White House, we have to take back the Senate, and we have to take back the House."[95]

Free people recoil from such control. The Progressives have been trying to introduce nationalized medicine in the United States for the last 80 years and a large majority of the public has consistently fought against it. Progressives who advocate more government control over health care decisions try to paint the failure to enact their agenda as a failure of our society. The real failure is their inability to understand or recognize that their schemes are not wanted or needed in a society of individuals who believe in personal responsibility. Health care is not a right: it is a commodity like housing, food, and clothing.

Progressives in both federal and state legislatures have already succeeded enough to endanger the remaining free market

---

[95] Breitbart TV: http://www.breitbart.tv/obama-in-03-id-like-to-see-a-single-payer-health-care-plan/

aspects of health care delivery in this country. Through unceasingly expanding Medicare and Medicaid, and by compensating doctors at a ridiculously low rate, government-run programs are effectively rationing care. The rising costs of the current system are a direct result of the laws and regulations Progressives have put in place that restrict the very free market forces that should moderate the expenses experienced by the consumer. Third party payments eliminate the incentive of the consumer to shop for the best care at the lowest cost.

Over the decades state legislatures have mandated various treatments and benefits that insurance companies must offer within their states, such as chiropractic care, acupuncture, and all manner of "alternative" medical practices. These laws naturally limit the number of insurance companies willing to comply with any specific states' standards. In California this has resulted in only six health insurance companies willing do to business in that state, out of over thirteen hundred companies in the United States. Progressives justify their final complete take-over of the medical field by the rising costs they have engineered. Nothing in the proposed legislation even mentions the rational free market solutions that are available, such as tort reform or allowing health insurance to be available across state lines.

Tort reform (capping punitive awards and disallowing frivolous individual and class-action lawsuits) would lower the high costs of liability insurance for hospitals and doctors. It would cut the costs of "defensive medicine", a practice of doctors to conduct a myriad of tests in order to protect themselves from potential, often groundless, lawsuits.

Allowing health insurance to be sold across state lines would offer more choice for Americans by increasing true competition between the insurance companies. This issue, for once, would be in accordance with the original intent of the Constitution's "commerce clause". If the governing elite truly wanted competition and lower costs, these are some of the easiest and most cost-effective ways to achieve the positive results they claim to support. Republican representatives submitted these and many other free market proposals as amendments, but Democrats voted against all of them in committee hearings.

Instead of common sense tort and insurance reforms, President Obama chose to slander the insurance companies by selling his "public option" as a way "to keep the insurance companies honest". He vilified doctors by claiming they remove tonsils unnecessarily to pad their fees and charge $50,000 to amputate a diabetic's foot rather than give the patient less lucrative life-style monitoring.[96] In regards to foot amputations, surgeons generally receive between $800 to $1,200 from Medicare and Medicaid for the surgery, a fee which also includes 90 days of follow-up care.

The initial cost estimates for the House health care plan are between $1 and 1.5 trillion. Lawmakers plan to cut $540 billion from Medicare and Medicaid and transfer these funds into the new federally regulated plan. They claim this money will not affect these established public programs because it will come from "cutting waste and fraud". If there is this much "waste and fraud" in these programs, why haven't these issues been addressed before funding a massive

---

[96] Obama statements at a press conference in July (tonsils), and New Hampshire Town Hall (surgeons) on August 11, 2009.

overhaul of the entire medical system? At a time when the Baby Boomer generation is entering their retirement years, and entitled to benefits they have paid for during their entire working lives, the federal government is planning on severely reducing the funding of these programs.

Despite the rush to pass this "urgently needed" bill, the legislation would not be implemented until 2013, well after the 2012 presidential election. In order to make the cost-benefit ratio more palatable to the public and moderate politicians, the funding for the plan was spread over ten years of tax collection for only seven years of actual service costs. In effect, taxes would be collected from the public for three years before any "benefits" of the plan would be available.

The regulation of health care goes beyond the scope of the enumerated powers of the federal government in the Constitution. This is an area reserved to the states and the people in the Tenth Amendment. It is also questionable whether the states would have any authority to mandate that free citizens purchase any form of private health insurance.

HR 3200 created a maze of 31 new bureaucratic agencies, offices, and commissions. (The total number eventually rose to 158.) Some of these new bureaucracies would include: Physician Quality Reporting Initiative (regulation of the treatments doctors can provide), Comparative Effectiveness Research Commission (regulation of the types of care provided to individuals based on their "quality of life"), and Health Choices Administration (regulation of benefits covered by private insurance companies).

Representative Kevin Brady (R-TX) and the Republican staff of the House Joint Economic Committee compiled a chart to demonstrate the organization of the Democrat sponsored health care plan.

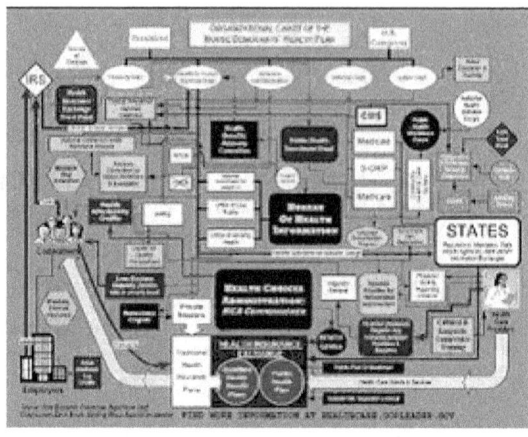

It resembles the pre-schoolers board games of "Candy Land" or "Chutes and Ladders". However, it is a serious illustration of the huge potential for "fraud and waste" that is inherent in all Progressive schemes to bilk the taxpayer of their money and control the citizen's right to freely choose how to live their life.

Democrat lawmakers in the House effectively blocked the distribution of this chart by claiming it was inaccurate, and therefore violated the rules on franked (free postage) mail sent by congressmen to their constituents.[97] Congressional rules prohibit comments in franked mails that are considered "partisan, politicized or personalized" when discussing pending legislation.

---

[97] _Roll Call_ "Democrats Block GOP Health Care Mailing" by Jackie Kucinich, July 23, 2009

Despite their efforts to squash the chart, it appeared on many Internet sites and was forwarded via email to millions of American citizens. Even as the Progressives caterwauled about "opposition lies", the majority party failed to submit a chart of their own to dispute the claimed inaccuracies.

Betsy McCaughey is a leader in the fight against nationalized medicine and takes the lead in providing accurate information to the public. McCaughy holds a Ph.D. in U.S. Constitutional History from Columbia University (1976), is the former Lt. Governor of New York (1995-98), a highly respected expert in health care policy, and her analysis of President Clinton's attempt to nationalize health care is credited for helping to defeat that plan.

She reads the bills, and her thorough analysis and understanding of legislative language enabled the public to engage in thoughtful and well-grounded debate with the proponents of government-controlled medicine. As opposition grew to the "public option", with many people seeing it as a step to a single-payer universal health care plan, President Obama flatly stated, "I have not said that I was a single-payer supporter".[98] This statement was made despite the widely distributed video of his appearance at the 2003 AFL-CIO conference cited above.

One of the most controversial debates has centered on what has become known as "death panels", as so aptly named by former Alaskan Governor Sarah Palin.[99] This moniker actually

---

[98] Presidential Town Hall meeting in Portsmouth, New Hampshire on August 11, 2009: http://www.washingtonexaminer.com/opinion/blogs/beltway-confidential/Obama-still-wont-come-clean-on-single-payer-52980182.html
[99] Sarah Palin, former Alaska Governor and Vice-Presidential candidate, comment on Facebook, August 7 and 12, 2009:

refers to the logical conclusion reached by understanding two different aspects of the bill and how they would inter-relate: First is the end-of-life counseling, and second is the establishment of the Comparative Effectiveness Research Commission.

The end-of-life counseling was detailed in Section 1233 of HR 3200, which states a medical provider (a doctor, physicians assistant, or a nurse practioner) shall perform the counseling once every five years for people over 65, or whenever the patient's health status changes, for example, after the diagnosis of a possibly terminal illness. "Shall" in the legislative world means "it's required". The practioner could initiate the subject of counseling without waiting for a patient request. Practioner performance would be rated, by government agencies, based on the percentage of patients that participate, thereby giving incentive to conduct end-of-life counseling to all patients that fall under the categories mandated in the legislation.

The legislation lists specific topics to be covered with the patient. These topics include identifying the patient's preference for various treatments at end-of-life, and putting in place powers of attorney and living wills. Also included is a directive to provide "suggested people to talk to", and "a list of national and state-specific resources".

Since the states of Oregon and Washington have legalized physician-assisted suicide, one must assume the topic would be part of the discussion in those states, at least initially. It is also possible that in these states the "suggested people to talk to" would include

http:www.facebook.com/note.php?not_id=113851103434 and
facebook.com/note.php?note_id=116471698434

Compassion and Choices, formerly known as the Hemlock Society, and Final Exit. These groups advocate for physician-assisted suicide and actively lobby for its adoption in the various states.

The Comparative Effectiveness Research Commission will rely on information provided by the already formed Federal Coordinating Council for Comparative Effectiveness Research that was included in the Stimulus Bill and funded with $1.1 billion. Comparative effectiveness research provides information on the relative strengths and weaknesses of various medical treatments and interventions. Measuring the effectiveness of treatments for various diagnoses has been used in countries with government-controlled health care as a cost saving device. Under the concepts known as "Quality Adjusted Life Years" or "Whole Life", comparisons are based on a person's disabilities versus a totally healthy person. Determinations are made regarding a patient's expected longevity and worth to society, and resources are rationed accordingly. The Commission's duties will include advocating health care treatments for individuals based on these systematic evaluations.

Dr. Ezekiel Emanuel, the brother of White House Chief of Staff Rahm Emanuel, is a member of the Federal Coordinating Council on Comparative Effectiveness Research. He is also a health policy advisor at the Office of Management and Budget, and contributed to the writing of the health care plan.

He has written, "Health services should not be guaranteed to individuals who are irreversibly prevented from being or becoming participating citizens. An obvious example is not guaranteeing health services to patients with dementia."[100]

---

[100] Hastings Center Report, Nov-Dec 1996

This policy advocates the denial of health services to those who are too ill, or disabled, to "participate" in society.

Betsy McCaughey stated, "Americans need to know what the president's health advisors have in mind for them." She continued, "No one has leveled with the public about these dangerous views."[101]

When Progressives argued that "death panels" were not in HR 3200, they were correct in so far as those two words do not appear anywhere in the bill. However, after combining the intentions of the end-of-life counseling and comparative effectiveness, any reasonable person must come to the conclusion that health care treatments will be rationed, or possibly denied, for the elderly and the disabled.

One of the many debated issues in HR 3200 was whether or not illegal immigrants would be a part of a national health plan. During committee mark-ups, Republican legislators tried numerous times to add amendments that specifically required proof of citizenship or legal residency status for access to all parts of the plan. The Democrat majorities on the committees defeated every one.

Progressive supporters liked to cite Section 246, which distributes "affordability credits" to people who can't afford to pay for their own health care insurance. This section states, "Nothing in this subtitle shall allow federal payments for affordability credits on behalf of individuals who are not lawfully present in the United States." This language applies only to the

---

[101] New York Post "Deadly Doctors" by Betsy McCaughey, July 24, 2009: http://www.nypost.com/p/news/opinion/opedcolumnists/deadly_doctors_PU6 Soiok2FbS368B7d7mAM

distribution of affordability credits subtitle, not to the entire bill. Couple this misdirection with the Progressives' known support for amnesty for illegal aliens, and it is clear that the estimated 20 million currently illegal immigrants in the United States will be covered by all functional aspects of the government-controlled health care program at taxpayers expense, with or without the affordability credits.

Among the many other troubling aspects of this bill are:

- Health insurance would be mandatory and individuals who choose not to enroll in a private or government plan would be fined,
- Business payroll taxes would be increased,
- Insurance companies would be prohibited from extending coverage to new customers,
- People with existing coverage would be prohibited from changing policies (except to enroll in the "public option"), and
- Doctor-patient confidentiality would be violated by computerized health records controlled by the government and made available to the newly created government panels and commissions.

Betsy McCaughey stated, "Members of congress haven't been reading this bill, and I think that's shameful."[102]

---

[102] New York Daily News "Former Lt. Gov. Betsy McCaughey Leads 'Death Panels' Charge Writing Up Talking Points" by David Saltonstall, August 12, 2009: http://www.nydailynews.com/news/2009/08/13/2009-08-13_former_lt_gov_mccaughey_leads_death_panel_charge_writing_up_talking_points

Just as Cap and Trade is not about saving the environment, the proposed government take-over of medicine was not about health care, but of controlling the people by controlling their medical decisions.

Californian and retired Registered Nurse, Gail Lightfoot, offered her alternative ideas to government-controlled health care, "Allow insurance companies to sell nationwide. Give employees a set amount of money and let them pick and choose the benefit they need. Make it easier to access safety net provisions so no one fails to use what is available. Get the government out of determining what services are allowed at what price."

Patriot citizen, Jeff Jarvis of Ohio, simply stated his opposition, "I didn't read the bill. I didn't have to. I do know that if congress exempts itself from the legislation, which they did, it is a bad deal."

Summing it all up, Gordon Rupp, a Tea Party Patriots coordinator in Stockton CA, stated, "Americans were asleep at the wheel as the Progressives had advanced their agenda from baby evolution steps to leaps and jumps. Inch by inch, step by step the Progressives have chipped away at our Constitution in their attempt to render it useless. And then came this shift in America. We citizens rapidly became educated about government and how it worked. We became so educated that we knew more about the bills being presented by the House and Senate than the politicians themselves."

Through the efforts of conservative groups like Tea Party Patriots, FreedomWorks, think-tank websites, and blogs, the American public was made aware of the horrendous pieces of legislation that were being considered and passed in congress. All of these groups, and many others, encouraged citizens to read these bills concocted by the elected officials. And read them they did. The resulting firestorm of opposition fueled attendance at Tea Party rallies, and caused a flurry of phone calls, letters, emails, and faxes to rain down on the elected officials ensconced in Washington.

When the representatives, from both parties, returned to their home districts for the traditional August recess a well-informed electorate was waiting for them at Town Hall meetings across the country.

Chapter Five

The Recess:
The Politicians Face The People

"Society in every state is a blessing,
but government even in its best state is but a necessary evil;
in its worst state an intolerable one;
for when we suffer, or are exposed to the same
miseries by a government,
which we might expect in a country without government,
our calamity is heightened by reflecting that we furnish the
means by which we suffer!"
- Thomas Paine, "Common Sense", 1776

Citizens responded to the arrogance of the non-representing representatives by actually reading the bills, or relevant portions of them, and educating themselves on the Progressive Movement and its history in American politics. Conservative books continued to dominate the best-seller lists, such as: *"Liberal Fascism"* by Jonah Goldberg, *"Liberty and Tyranny"* by Mark Levin, *"Common Sense"* by Glenn Beck, and many others. (Readers are encouraged to read these and other books to gain a fuller understanding of the goals and ideology of Progressivism.)

Conservative authors helped everyday people to recognize the socialist influences in the Progressive policies and programs undermining our Constitution and our rights as citizens. The people began to understand the ways in which the political class had been slowly leading America away from liberty and individualism, and towards a collective society. It did not matter which political party held power; Democrat or Republican, the only difference seemed to be the scope and speed of their programs and spending.

With the implementation of the radical Progressive agenda hounding us on all sides, more and more Americans are learning and understanding that collectivist policies, practiced by both political parties, are the antithesis of our Constitution. As our fiery founder, Patrick Henry, stated before the Continental Congress, "The Constitution is not an instrument for government to restrain the people, it is an instrument for the people to restrain the government, lest it come to dominate our lives and interests." A true republic is based on the free actions of an educated and independent citizen. However, Progressive policies always punish the productive, drive away business, investment, jobs, and enslave people to dependence upon government handouts and criminal sub-cultures.

Take a look at the cities and states that have been governed for the last forty years by Progressives. The once great cities of Chicago, Detroit, and Washington D.C., along with once productive states like Illinois, Michigan, Massachusetts, and now California, are stark examples of the implementation of Progressive policies. These metropolises and sovereign states are bankrupt and moral failures. However, to Progressives their policies are successful because they weaken the great American economic engine, and accrue tremendous power and wealth to the ruling elite.

The real world results are corrupt cities where regulations choke free enterprise, and overbearing bureaucracies interfere in everyday life through an endless array of projects and strategic plans. People are channeled into programs where they can be corralled, controlled, and warehoused. But, perhaps even more important, people are robbed of their personal power to use their creativity and freedom to build the successful, personal economic foundation on which the nation depends.

Feeling comfortable with their new total federal power, the Progressives pulled out of back drawers every free market busting policy or program they had ever dreamed up. Expecting the usual token resistance from the Republican Party, they assumed their anti-capitalist schemes would sail through the legislative process and become law overnight.

The last thing they expected was resistance from the American people. With a forty-year's dominance, by their own design, of education, news media, and entertainment, the Progressives assumed they had so cowed the general public that the final take-down of America would be accomplished with little effort. They assured themselves that the silent majority was passing away with the WWII generation, and its influence was a myth from a bygone era. And perhaps, if they had stayed their course of employing incremental change, they may have achieved their goal to end the great American experiment in government by the governed.

However, blinded by the arrogance of their anti-Americanism, they had no knowledge or understanding of the existence of an innate American spirit — a spirit that refused to

154

even conceive of the idea that individual liberty would vanish from this land. This spirit was aroused in the heart of the silent majority and it compelled them, even thinking they may be alone, out into the street to reassert their sovereignty over their elected officials. And, there in the street with them were other same-minded folks who had also ended their silence and were hungry for the truth.

Modern patriots have come to understand that the greatest threat to all totalitarian-based regimes is an educated citizenry. They are learning about Progressivism as the source of current policies, and are trying to keep up with the latest legislation brewing in the U.S. Senate and House of Representatives. Patriots are using the Internet to research policy initiatives and track the connections between politicians and Progressive advocacy groups, and are forwarding that information to friends and contacts through emails, posting on blogs, and connecting through Facebook and Twitter. They share what they learn with their family and friends.

It does not take much study for true Americans, native born or immigrant, to understand the freedoms guaranteed in the Constitution, and in that light to respond to the dangers posed to a free society by the long-term ramifications of Progressivism. A year ago the average mom talked about the latest movies, school activities, and fashion; today the talk is about congressmen who are oblivious to public opinion, deliberate government take-overs of private industries, and Progressive anti-capitalist propaganda imbedded in school curriculum. A year ago they would have chalked up such talk as "conspiracy theories", but today these are the reasonable concerns of an average person.

Tea Party people and 9.12'ers also share with each other the philosophy of our founding fathers. The rediscovered wisdom of the founders is a joy for the modern patriots, who sprinkle their communications with quotations from our political fathers such as John Adams, James Madison, Thomas Jefferson, and George Washington. Far from being the musty musings of the long dead, they are as prescient today as when first spoken, and provide both warnings and advice on how patriots should proceed during our current political crisis.

Town Hall meetings have been part of the American political landscape since Colonial times. Where once citizens voted on governing initiatives, Town Halls now serve as the forum for constituents to communicate in person with their elected representatives. Until the Tea Party summer of 2009, congressional representatives were lucky to have 50 citizens attend a district meeting, and that, only if they spoke at the senior center after Bingo on Wednesday afternoon. Attendance at public meetings began to swell in June and July in response to the Stimulus Bill, auto industry bailouts, the Cap & Trade Bill, and the Health care reform bill. Hundreds to thousands of citizens began to show up, and it became readily apparent they were better versed in the particulars of the legislation than the non-representing representatives.

The Internet buzzed as various websites reported real-time information about the Town Hall meetings from bloggers and posters who were participating or giving "after action" reports and downloading videos. Most described large crowds who were unfailingly polite to each other as they waited, and were energized about having the opportunity to communicate with their congressman without the buffer provided by protective staff.

It became common for the citizens to get vocal when the representatives tried to answer their questions with boilerplate quotes from the party leadership. Most of the elected officials appeared to be flummoxed at being confronted with a skeptical audience. A poster on the website Lucianne.com commented on a district "coffee" they attended with Representative Henry Cuellar (D-TX). "We have been at these coffees before and have never seen such a vocal, in-his-face crowd at one of these meetings. There were even demonstrators which we've never seen. These representatives better realize it is not business as usual with the home folks."[103]

One of the first elected officials to experience the new era of watchful citizenship was Representative Tim Bishop (D-NY), at a Town Hall held in Setauket on June 22nd. The center-left Politico website reported, "protesters dominated the meeting by shouting criticisms at the congressman for his positions". Within an hour the congressman called the police to escort him to his car, and subsequently cancelled any other events in his Long Island district. "I had felt they would be pointless," Bishop stated. "There is no point in meeting with my constituents and listen to them and have

---

[103] "pjpblush" as posted on www.lucianne.com on July 27, 2009.

them listen to you if what is basically an unruly mob prevents you from having an intelligent conversation."[104]

The attempt to label citizens showing up at Town Halls as "unruly mobs" became fashionable with Progressive politicians in an attempt to nullify the people's concerns. An Internet poster proclaimed, "Let it be known that the public 'mob' cannot pass laws to take away our liberties and steal our money for their frivolous power grabs. The congressional mob is the one to be feared. Our vote is our weapon."[105]

While canceling Town Hall meetings became a popular avoidance tactic for some members of the political class, other representatives deployed the use of "telephone town halls" to accomplish their constituent outreach. Using the telephone as a venue allowed congressional staff to screen the callers and the politician to answer a set of pre-selected questions. Representatives used this method as either an adjunct to the public meeting or as a substitute altogether. Other avoidance tactics included setting up meetings in remote locations with little notice, packing meetings with Progressive-minded union members, and presenting panels of "experts" that left little time for constituent questions. It is estimated about one third of congressional representatives held no open public meetings in their districts during the summer recess. So, for those representatives who toughed it out, some recognition is due for at least showing up.

---

[104] Politico article, "Town Halls Gone Wild" by Alex Isenstadt, posted on Yahoo! News July 31, 2009:
http://news.yahoo.com/s/politico/20090731/pl_politico/25646/
[105] "rinktum" as posted on www.lucianne.com, August 4, 2009, thread #485939.

In late June, at a Town Hall in Panama City FL with Representative Allen Boyd (D), one hundred sign-carrying protesters turned up, while at a meeting in Danville VA with Congressman Thomas Perriello (D), some participants claimed they were prevented from displaying their signs and were escorted out of the meeting by plain-clothes security. Freshman Congressman Dan Maffei (D-NY) faced a spirited crowd at a middle school in Syracuse, as well as veteran three-term Congressman Russ Carnahan (D-MO) who was heckled at his St. Louis Town Hall. Representative Mike Castle of Delaware, one of the eight Republicans to vote in favor of Cap & Trade, was confronted with a capacity crowd asking detailed questions about his energy policies. [106] The ubiquitous question asked by citizens everywhere was, "Did you read the bill?"

On July 27th, House Judiciary Chairman John Conyers (D-MI) made a revealing comment about that point during a speech at the National Press Club. Obviously comfortable in the setting, a laughing Conyers began, "I love these members, they get up and say, 'Read the bill'." He then mocked, "What good is reading the bill if it's a thousand pages and you don't have two days and two lawyers to find out what it means after you read the bill?"

Conyers comments, and his casual presentation, are indicative of his high level of comfort in voting for Progressive legislation. Not only are his nonchalance and arrogance astounding, but so also the silence of most of his fellow congress members showing they're comfortable with that same outlook.

---

[106] Politico article, "Town Halls Gone Wild" by Alex Isenstadt, posted on Yahoo! News July 31, 2009:
http://news.yahoo.com/s/politico/20090731/pl_politico/25646/

This attitude was an insult to every patriot and it galvanized the determination of the Tea Party people and Town Hall participants. Citizens began to demand that elected representatives actually know and understand legislation before they vote on it. Many believed it was past time for the politicians to be held accountable for their policies and their spending.

It was not just elected officials who faced informed citizens. The American Association for Retired Persons (AARP) was one of the organizations running TV advertisements favorable to health care reform. They, too, were holding open meetings for their membership.

An Internet poster reported, "Just came back from an AARP town hall style meeting. The person leading the meeting gave a brief talk & took questions. The people who asked questions were contradicting the answers the AARP person gave. Then a few people got excited (NOT shouting) in their replies so the AARP person said, 'Let me just rush this so we can,' and someone yelled, 'NO! We don't want to be rushed! That's just one problem with this healthcare reform package.' The AARP person laughed & said this has been in the works since the 1990s. The seniors countered her every comment so she walked out of the meeting and tried to get the rec center to make everyone leave. The AARP members refused to leave and held their own meeting and planning session. The worm is turning folks!"[107]

This new era of informed citizens even compelled the Democrat leadership to give specific guidance and advice to its younger members. On July 28th there was a meeting for freshman

---

[107] "pouncer" posted on www.lucianne.com, August 4, 2009

lawmakers, led by Congressman Chris Van Hollen (D-MD) chair of the Democratic Congressional Campaign Committee. Also invited to this meeting were officials from Organizing for America, the post-election incarnation of Obama's campaign structure of paid staffers and volunteers.[108]

According to "one House Democrat leadership aide" familiar with the meeting, the topic of Town Hall protesters did not specifically come up, but Van Hollen is reported to have said, "Go on offense. Stay on the offense. It's really important that your constituents hear directly from you. You shouldn't let a day go by that your constituents don't hear from you."[109] There appears to be no mention of actually "listening to your constituents" as a point of discussion in this meeting.

Another Internet poster observed, "Yep, passions are rising. Dems are shocked that Republicans, Conservatives would actually show up and demand answers when they are ramming legislation down our throats that will forever change this nation and not for the better. You are seeing real freedom loving Americans standing up to tyranny and we're not backing down. We're fighting for the very soul of this nation." [110]

––––––––––––––––

The Obama administration was fighting for single-payer, socialized medicine. In order to still the restless crowds they sent

––––––––––––––––

[108] Los Angeles Times "Obama's Grass Roots Network is Put to the Test" by Peter Wallsten, August 10, 2009: http://www.latimes.com/features/health/la-na-health-grassroots10-2009aug10,0,664834
[109] Politico article, "Town Halls Gone Wild" by Alex Isenstadt, posted on Yahoo! News July 31, 2009:
http://news.yahoo.com/s/politico/20090731/pl_politico/25646/
[110] "beat the press" posted on www.lucianne.com, August 4, 2009.

out Health and Human Services Secretary Kathleen Sebelius to a Town Hall accompanied by Republican-turned-Democrat Senator Arlen Specter (PA). On Sunday, August 2nd, they appeared together in Philadelphia at the National Constitution Center. (I imagine that the irony of this venue selection was lost on the staffer who made the arrangements.)

According to Associated Press writer, Kimberly Hefling, they "faced an antagonistic, standing-room-only crowd," that "booed, jeered and occasionally cheered in a raucous session."[111] A popular video on You Tube shows a decidedly uncomfortable Sebelius, as pale as her cream colored suit, standing in disbelief that administration policies should even be questioned. Specter, an old campaigner, handled the crowd better, but his eyes betrayed astonishment at the widespread opposition.[112]

One of the questions put forward came from a woman who asked, "How can you manage health care when you can't even manage 'Cash for Clunkers'?" The crowd responded with an approving roar. (The "Cash for Clunkers" program was a "stimulus" idea to jump start failing auto sales. With an offer of $4,500 trade-in value for a "gas guzzler" towards a new car, hundreds of thousands of vehicles were sold in less than a week. The new cars often achieved only a few miles-per-gallon more than the replacement. Three billion dollars, that was supposed to support the program for two months, was blown out in four days. The real-

---

[111] Yahoo! News article "Public Passions are Rising on Health Care Overhaul" by Kimberly Hefling, on August 3, 2009: http://news.yahoo.com/s/ap/20090804/ap_on_go_co/us_health_care_overhaul/
[112] You Tube Video "How Can You Manage Health Care When You Can't Manage Cash for Clunkers?": http://www.youtube.com/watch?v=cpt8BzyFpa4&feature=related

world consequence was the removal from the market of good second-hand vehicles, as all the "clunkers" were sent to the scrap yard.)

After a week of Democrats, and their Progressive minions in the press, highlighting the most contentious Town Hall interactions, the White House began to intensify the denial and denigration of legitimate citizen concerns. On August 4th, Press Secretary Robert Gibbs implied that the opposition to the health care bill was organized by a small group trying to create "manufactured anger". He continued, "I hope people will take a jaundiced eye to what is clearly the Astroturf nature of so-called grassroots lobbying."

Gibbs continued with a comparison of the protesters to the "Brooks Brothers Brigade" he claimed appeared during the Florida recount after the Bush-Gore presidential election. He intimated, "I seem to see some commonality in who pops up at some of these things. You can see quite a bit of similarity between who shows up where."[113] This comment echoed Senator Barbara Boxer's remarks just two days earlier on MSNBC's "Hardball" with Chris Matthews, when she offered, as proof of the Astroturf nature of the rallies, her observation that Tea Partiers are "too well dressed".

Later that day, Democratic National Committee spokesman, Brad Woodhouse described the Town Hall citizens as "angry mobs of rabid right-wing extremists". He concluded, "Much like we saw at the McCain-Palin rallies last year, where crowds were baited with cries of 'socialist', 'communist', and

---

[113] The Wall Street Journal "White House Isn't Concerned by Health-Care Protests" by Henry J. Pulizzi, August 4, 2009:
http://online.wsj.com/article/SB124939676158504833.html

where the birthers movement was born, these mobs of extremists are not interested in having a thoughtful discussion about the issues."

"Birthers" is a derogatory term used by Progressives to describe a significant number of citizens who question if Barack Obama is a legitimate natural-born citizen of the United States. Their concerns are based on Obama's refusal to make public his original long-form Birth Certificate, or release his application and educational records for Occidental College, Columbia University, and Harvard University. Also missing from the public domain are his office records during the time he was an Illinois State Senator.

On August 4th, the Obama administration announced a website that would be a clearinghouse for debunking supposed rumors and myths about the health care bill. White House senior advisor, David Axelrod stated, "We are going to be very aggressive. The last thing we want to do is let misimpressions fester because we were laggard in responding."[114]

Macon Phillips, Obama's Director of New Media, presented the "Facts Are Stubborn Things" website rollout on the White House Blog Post. The first video featured Linda Douglass, the Communications Director for the White House Health Reform Office. Prior to her taking that position, Ms. Douglass was the reporter covering the Obama presidential campaign for ABC News. The video featured attempts to reinforce Obama's claim that if a person liked their current insurance plan they could keep it.

---

[114] Politico article, "W.H. Launches Attacks on Attacks" by Carrie Budoff Brown, August 4, 2009: http://dyn/politico.com/printstory.cfm?uuid=E7E04E09-18Fe-70B2-A8EBB42AC81CC07D

After the video there was a dark and disturbing turn in this posting. It was the call for Americans to spy on each other and report "fishy" comments. Phillips wrote, "There is a lot of disinformation about health insurance reform out there, spanning from control of personal finances to end-of-life care. These rumors often travel just below the surface via chain emails or through casual conversation. Since we can't keep track of all of them here at the White House, we're asking for your help. If you get an email or see something on the web about health insurance reform that seems fishy, send it to flag@whitehouse.gov."[115]

It was not long before the new email address at the White House became derisively known as the "Fishtapo" on websites popular with Tea Party people and other constitutionalists. Conservative posters across the blogosphere were "turning themselves in" as opponents of the president's plans, and calls went out over websites to overload the White House "Fishtapo" inbox. In response to the request that the White House be alerted to "something fishy", many posters downloaded and sent the entire text of HR 3200. Knowing that the huge file would eat-up bandwidth on the White House computer servers just added to the fun.

Senator John Cornyn (R-TX) told Fox News, "No one expects that when they exercise their First Amendment rights to ask questions or complain about a proposed government program that they're going to be listed on a database in the White House." He also said the White House effort raises privacy concerns, "You

---

[115] The White House Blog Post "Facts Are Stubborn Things" by Macon Phillips, August 4, 2009: http://www.whitehouse.gov/blog/facts-are-stubborn-things/

don't have to be a conspiracy theorist to see the potential for serious abuse."[116]

In the days following the introduction of the "Fishtapo", the Obama Administration faced increasing opposition from conservative groups calling this action reminiscent of President Nixon's infamous "enemies list". There were even rumblings from some members of the establishment press. However, the most persistent questioner was Major Garrett from Fox News. On August 13th, Garrett reported he had received information from many people about emails sent to them from presidential special advisor, David Axelrod. The subject was debunking the "myths" surrounding Obama's health care reform package. None of these people had ever accessed the White House website for any purpose, and especially not to ask questions about the health care reform "myths". Garrett repeatedly asked how Axelrod got the email addresses of these people, if not from "flag@whitehouse.gov". Gibbs deflected the question without answering.

Garrett pressed the issue with Secretary Gibbs for several days, with the White House giving a different answer each day. On August 17th, the "Fishtapo" email account was shut down.

Besides setting up their informant network, during the first days of August the Obama White House also took measures to organize their own "mob" to counter the presence of patriotic

---

[116] Fox News "Critics Accuse White House of Playing 'Big Brother' in Health Care Debate, August 6, 2009:
http://www.foxnews.com/politics/2009/08/06/critics-accuse-white-house-playing-big-brother-health-care-debate/

citizens. A coordinated message began to be sent out by organizations close to President Obama.

John Sweeny, head of the powerful AFL-CIO union, described the Town Halls as the "principal battleground" in the health care fight and announced he would be sending union members to counter critics. One must wonder if union members were to attend Town Halls as interested parties or as "security"?

The presidential campaign structure, "Obama for America", consisted of a network of paid staffers, volunteers, trained organizers, and a 13 million-strong email list. The organization was retained and put under the reputed control of the Democratic National Committee, and is known by its new name "Organizing for America" (OFA). Mitch Stewart, OFA Executive Director, sent an email with directions for dealing with any hostile conservative presence at Town Halls and neutralizing their impact. He relayed the Democrat counter-attack to citizen concerns, "The goal of these disruptions is for a few people to get a lot of media attention and hijack the entire public discourse."[117]

Health Care for America Now (HCAN), a massive umbrella organization that represents the lobbying efforts of Progressive organizations and unions such as MoveOn, the NAACP, and the SEIU, sent out their own, more detailed Town Hall instructions to their minions. They were advised to coordinate meeting strategies with congressional aides before the event, arrive hours before possible opponents to gather "in the

---

[117] CNN Political Ticker "Liberal Groups Launch Town Hall Counteroffensive" by Rebecca Sinderband, August 6, 2009: http://politicalticker.blogs.cnn.com/2009/08/06/liberal-groups-launch-town-hall-counteroffensive/

front to create a wall around the member", and assign individuals to shadow reporters and "be assertive in shaping the narrative."

The instructions also included "precautions to make sure that you can keep meetings you organize under control". The guidelines included ensuring attendees are "easily identifiable", establishing a strictly controlled question-asking procedure, and banning or collecting any signs and leaflets not issued by meeting organizers. They were also instructed to assign marshals to keep the crowd organized and orderly, and to act as security when noisy or disruptive protesters are asked to leave.[118]

That same week job advertisements began to appear on Craig's List, an Internet classified ads website, looking for "talented leaders needed to work for health care reform", and "job opportunities working on grassroots campaigns". The jobs paid $11 to $16 per hour, and were offered by an organization with a website titled JobsThatMatter.[119]

It appears that "Astroturf" is in the eye of the beholder. ABC News caught up with Speaker of the House Nancy Pelosi in a crowded Capitol hallway on August 5th. The reporter asked, "Do you think there's legitimate grassroots opposition going on here?"

Pelosi imperially stated, "I think they are Astroturf." She sneered, "You be the judge, they're carrying swastika and symbols like that to a town meeting on healthcare."[120] No photos have ever

---

[118] Health Care for America NOW! Website "Fight Back Against The Right", August 2009: http://healthcareforamericanow.org/site/fight
[119] Craigs List website for New York, August 2009: http://newyork.craigslist.org/mnh/etc/1303066561.html
[120] Video taken from the Fox News broadcast of the *O'Rielly Factor*, posted on Real Clear Politics website, August 5, 2009: http://www.realclearpolitics.com/video/2009/08/05/pelosi-town-hall-protesters-are-carrying-swastikas.html

been produced that show "swastika" being prevalent at Tea Party rallies or Town Hall meetings.

The next day, when Senate Majority Leader Harry Reid was asked about the grassroots nature of the protesters, he scoffed while he held aloft his prop—a piece of artificial turf, "These are nothing more than destructive efforts to interrupt a debate that we should have, and are having." Apparently Senator Reid failed to understand that the protesters were actually trying to debate the issues with their representatives.

Reid continued, "They are doing this because they don't have any better ideas. They have no interest in letting the negotiators, even though few in number negotiate. It's really simple: they're taking their cues from talk show hosts, Internet rumor-mongers, and insurance rackets."[121]   (The Senate Finance Committee had six members, three from each party, that were negotiating separately from the full committee about which aspects of the House health care bill to include in the Senate version. Eventually all free market solutions offered by Republican senators were voted down by the Democrat majority.)

That same day, President Obama sent a special email message to the 13 million on OFA's contact list. He wrote, "There are those who profit from the status quo or see this debate as a political game, and they will stop at nothing to block reform. They are filling the airwaves and the Internet with outrageous falsehoods to scare people into opposing change." This message is an example of

---

[121] St. Louis Post-Dispatch "Six People, Including P-D Reporter, Arrested at Carnahan Meeting" by Leah Thorsen, august 6, 2009: http://www.stltoday/emaf.nsf/Popup?ReadForm&db=stltoday%5Cnews%5Cs tories.nsf&doci…

the typical Progressive response: demonize the opposition and accuse them of the very motives and tactics you yourself are using — classic "double-speak".

All of this effort was expended in order to refute the genuine opposition of the American people. The actions of the Obama administration and Democrat congressional representatives appeared to validate the concerns of many Americans that the political class was determined to rob them of their individual sovereignty and enslave generations to come under an oppressive central regime.

––––––––––––––––––

Within days of HCAN's and the union's call-out to man the health care barricades against the citizen protesters, the first incidents of violence occurred at two Town Hall meetings on the evening of August 6th.

Folks had begun to line up early, and eventually over 1,000 people gathered for the meeting with Congressman Russ Carnahan (D-MO) at the Bernard Middle School gym in south St. Louis County.[122] Witnesses reported that between one and two hundred people, wearing purple SEIU shirts, arrived in several buses and were immediately escorted into the meeting venue through a back door. People at the front of the line said that the room was already half full when the main doors were finally opened.

The line for the meeting followed the interior school hallway, about four abreast, towards a set of double metal doors that led into the gym. The doors were only open a short time before

––––––––––––––––––

[122] Ibid.

several large men, wearing union ID tags, closed them. Citizens in the hallway responded by shouting and banging. After some time of registering their complaint, they joined the others waiting outside.

The overflow crowd stayed while the meeting took place. There was a mixture of supporters and protesters of the health care plan, with people interacting with each other in spirited debate. It was an ongoing combination of one-on-one discussions and groups trying to out-chant each other. Good old-fashioned American political discourse.

One of those in the crowd was Kenneth Gladney, a 38-year-old conservative activist from St. Louis. He was handing out small "Don't Tread On Me" flags to the crowd when the meeting ended and the gym began to empty out. Suddenly, two large men in SEIU purple t-shirts approached the slightly built Gladney. Both of them were black men and called Gladney, also a black man, "nigger", before one of them punched him in the face. The second attacker pulled him by his shirt collar over the table, down to the ground and began kicking him. With Gladney on the ground, the second attacker joined in the beating. Quickly responding, several white men ran to Gladney's defense and put themselves between him and his attackers. Other men then surrounded the attackers, standing around them shoulder to shoulder, until a police car was flagged down and the SEIU men were arrested.

Kenneth Gladney was taken to St. John's Mercy Medical Center where he was treated for injuries to his knee, back, elbow, shoulder and face. He was kept overnight. "It just seems there's no freedom of speech without being attacked," he said.[123] Conservative blacks face particular persecution for their political beliefs because the collectivist left assumes it owns every black vote. Blacks who espouse individualist thinking are the run-a-ways from the modern Progressive plantation, and they are treated as such.

In a prepared statement released the next morning, Representative Carnahan said, "Sadly we've seen stories about disrupters around the country, and we have a handful of them here in Missouri. Instead of participating in a civil debate, they have mobilized with special interests in Washington who have lined their pockets by overcharging Americans for a broken health care system." Apparently, Mr. Carnahan believes Mr. Gladney beat himself up.

On Saturday, August 8th, the St. Louis Tea Party held a press conference and peaceable protest at the SEIU headquarters in St. Louis. The protest was to demand justice and denounce the violence suffered by Kenneth Gladney. Approximately 100 protesters, including Mr. Gladney in a wheelchair, were present. The _St. Louis Post Dispatch_ covered the story.

The identical scenario of St. Louis also played out in Tampa FL on August 6th, at Congresswoman Kathy Castor's (D) Town Hall. Approximately 1,500 people were lined up outside waiting for the front doors to open, while SEIU and ACORN

---

[123] St. Louis Post-Dispatch "Six People, Including P-D Reporter, Arrested at Carnahan Meeting" by Leah Thorsen, august 6, 2009: http://www.stltoday/emaf.nsf/Popup?ReadForm&db=stltoday%5Cnews%5Cstories.nsf&doci...

members were ushered in through the back door and took their reserved seats in the front of the conference room.

When the doors opened, only about 75 people were let into the room, including those who could fit standing against the walls. The doors remained opened and people stood shoulder to shoulder in the small enclave-hallway off a main lobby area.

At one point, in reaction to a Castor comment the crowd began to chant, "You work for us!" Plain clothes "security" started to push people back past the doors. There was confusion when a woman was separated from her elderly father, she being inside the conference room and he still in the hallway. As the doors were closing a man tried to help the older man and was thrown against the wall by one of the "sergeant at arms". The man's shirt was torn. The doors were closed. The crowd began chanting, "Hear our voice"!

It was reported that outside the meeting, protester Randy Arthur was beaten by suspected union thugs.[124] An Internet poster observed, "There have been no assaults or injuries until Obama calls out his troops and suddenly we have racial slurs against black conservatives and assaults."[125]

─────────────

At a meeting in Des Moines IA on August 8th with Senator Tom Harkin (D) several participants shouted criticisms. Harkin stated he didn't expect Iowans to take part in "scare tactics, misinformation and obstruction." He continued, "As we have

─────────────

[124] American Thinker "Chicago Thug Tactics" by Pamela Geller, August 9, 2009: http://www.americanthinker.com/blog/2009/08/chicago_thug_tactics/
[125] "GOPLady" on www.lucianne.com, August 7, 2009.

seen in recent days, opponents are pulling out all stops to kill the reform effort. This is a shame."

A man from the audience yelled, "This is not health reform, this is control, control over our lives." Harkin responded, "As I said, there is a nationally coordinated effort to disrupt these meetings". The man shot back, "No one sent me to this meeting!"[126]

On Monday, August 10th, House Speaker Nancy Pelosi (D-CA) and House Majority Whip Steny Hoyer (D-MD) attempted to silence dissent, but instead stoked the flames, with an op-ed piece for *USA Today* entitled, "Un-American Attacks Can't Derail Health Care Debate". They cynically wrote, "The dialogue between elected representatives and constituents is at the heart of our democracy and plays an integral role in assuring that the legislation we write reflects the genuine needs and concerns of the people we represent."

Pelosi and Hoyer then went on the attack, "However, it is now evident that an ugly campaign is underway not merely to misrepresent the health insurance reform legislation, but to disrupt public meetings and prevent members of congress and constituents from conducting a civil dialogue. These disruptions are occurring because opponents are afraid not just of differing views — but of the facts themselves. Drowning out opposing views is simply un-American."[127]

---

[126] Fox News "Outbursts, Hot Tempers Fill Town Hall Meetings Across U.S." by Associated Press, August 8, 2009:
http://www.foxnews.com/politics/2009/08/08/outbursts-hot-tempers-town-hall-meetings/
[127] USA Today "Un-American Attacks Can't Derail Health Care Debate" by Nancy Pelosi and Steny Hoyer, August 10, 2009:

In response, Brian Walsh of the National Republican Senatorial Committee said, "It's interesting to see the President's political machine calling on his supporters to use their Constitutional right to free speech when the White House spent the last week criticizing others for doing the exact same thing." He continued, "Republicans agree that every American should have the right to voice their opinion in a calm, respectful manner but after the 'astroturfing' rhetoric from the Democrats this week, it's hard to ignore the hypocrisy."[128]

On the ground, the president's political machine seemed to be stalling. Ten days into the crucial month of August, the _Los Angeles Times_ reported that the famed Organizing for America network was faltering. Peter Wallsten wrote, "the group is still figuring out how to operate," and that "work has been slowed by tensions over tactics, disenchantment among some core supporters and an effective GOP resistance."

Wallsten's article told the story of several OFA supporters, including Beth Kimbriel in Chester, Virginia. Kimbriel volunteers up to 40 hours a week "trying to persuade locals to support Obama". However, the critics of the health care plan that were spreading what she called "misinformation" stymied her. When she tries to explain Obama's policy positions, Kimbriel complained she finds, "It's difficult to be believed."

http://blogs.usatoday.com/oped/2009/08/unamerican-attacks-cant-derail-health-care-debate-.html

[128] ABC News "Painting Protestors as 'Partisan Mobs with Lies About Health Reform' Democrats Rally Their Own Activists to Visit Members of Congress at Town Halls, District Offices" by Jake Tapper, August 9, 2009: http://blogs.abcnews.com/politicalpunch/2009/08/painting-protestors-as-partisan-mobs-with-lies-about-health-reform/

Others were still waiting to be told what to do. Candice Davies, of Cary NC, trained canvassers for Obama's presidential campaign and was trying to organize support for the health care plan. She observed that last year, "Obama's sexy, he was hot, and everybody wanted a piece of that. Now, people are going to have to work for something that is not quite as slick or sexy." She said she had attended an OFA organizational meeting but came away "without any clear script or anything to do." She reported that OFA "hasn't contacted me with a really clear mission. If they came to my door and said, 'Here are the 10 things we want you to do,' then I'd probably do it."

Another resident of Cary, Murray Silverstone, said he was inspired by the election and eager to help with the health care fight. He wondered why OFA staffers didn't arrive in his area to organize the campaign until 5 weeks prior, "It wasn't clear to us why there was such a delay."

Reporter Wallsten observed, "One complication is that activists are being asked to sell an evolving plan; even Obama hasn't committed to details". Silverstone and his wife began canvassing and talking to individuals about supporting Obama's health care reform, but then switched to just using petitions provided by OFA that laid out the president's broader policies. Silverstone opined, "OFA should try to focus on one detail, like the public option, that people can really identify with."

Organizing for America began to address the concerns of the network members who remained active, and supplemented their ranks with professional field organizers and trained volunteers. Jeremy Bird, OFA Deputy Director, said they had hired staffers in 42 states and expected to have paid workers in every state within a matter of weeks. [129]

This article presents evidence of one of the most fundamental differences between Progressivism and traditional American individualism: Those who believe in the supremacy of the collective need others to tell them what to do, and those who believe in the primacy of the individual do not. The battle lines are not drawn between political party disputes, but rather more profoundly, between ideologies. Between Collectivism and Individualism. Between tyranny and liberty.

As a poster on Lucianne.com aptly observed, "The liberals characterize what is happening in town hall meetings across the country as a 'campaign', suggesting a tightly organized effort by conservatives. In actuality, this outcry cuts across party lines because it affects everyone, and the Democrats' strategy of attacking those who are speaking out against this travesty, thinking they are only conservatives, will come back to haunt them in a huge way."[130]

On August 10th the Rasmussen survey released data regarding the attitudes of Americans towards the proposed health care legislation. Likely voters were asked whether they favored a single-payer health care system. The response showed 57% rejected government-controlled medicine to 32% in favor. Interestingly, the party breakdown showed the deep chasm between Progressives and mainstream Americans.

---

[129] Los Angeles Times "Obama's Grass-roots Network is Put to the Test" by Peter Wallsten, August 10, 2009: http://www.latimes.com/features/health/la-na-health-grassroots10-2009aug10,0,664834
[130] "hardhead" posted on www.lucianne.com, August 10, 2009.

Most Democrats, 62%, support single-payer health care, but that still left a sizable minority of 38% of the party either opposed or uncommitted. Others overwhelmingly resist socialized medicine: a decisive 87% of Republicans reject the proposal, and Independents oppose it by 63% to 22%.[131]

Democrat politicians put themselves in an untenable position. They sold, too well, the Progressive snake oil to their hard-left base. They had no way to truthfully present their "public option" to an ever growing number of skeptical citizens, who realized that the proposed government-run system would lead to the rationing of services to, and discrimination against, the disabled and the elderly. The American people understood the moral difference between dictatorial government mandates and millions of people making their own free choices.

Power Line blogger John Hinderaker wrote, "I suspect that the Democrats' inability to talk honestly about health care (in public, anyway) is part of what drives their hysteria in the face of opposition to their plans."[132]

Another observer of the political scene, Andrew Breitbart, elaborated, "But the mockery. The recklessness. Unsupportable libel isn't working. The tea parties and, now, the health care protests at town-hall meetings have only gotten bigger and stronger. The anti-big-government movement is pure. Its participants represent something close to what used to be considered normative in this country."

[131] Power Line Blog "The Democrats' Dilemma" by John Hinderaker, August 10, 2009: http://www.powerlineblog.com/archives/2009/08/024242.php
[132] Ibid.

He continued, "Tea Party attendees and health care town-hall protesters share a common belief that the extravagant spending of President Obama and the Democrat Party – absent any checks and balances – will eventually lead more people into government dependency, higher taxes and, perhaps, our country's financial ruin. These are legitimate fears felt by millions of Americans."

Breitbart concluded, "That's why the media and the Democrat Party are scared and are throwing outrageous and hateful accusations at everyday Americans — hoping that people stay home out of fear."[133]

An Internet poster put it a little more succinctly, "With Obama it is 'grassroots network'…with conservative opposition it is 'Nazi-like Mobs'. Anyone else see the hypocrisy here?"[134]

On August 12th Representative Susan Davis (D-CA) held a Town Hall in the northern San Diego County area. A report from a citizen participant stated that the meeting had been "taken over by the SEIU and Organizing for America. Several buses arrived and as the passengers got off they were each given their commercially printed sign. They were lead by obviously experienced activists — who inquired of our grassroots citizen group, 'Where were you bused in from?'"[135]

---

[133] The Washington Times "BREITBART: I Am Kenneth Gladney" by Andrew Breitbart, August 10, 2009:
http://www.washingtontimes.com/news/2009/aug/10/i-am-kenneth-gladney/
[134] "Aggie57" posted on www.lucianne.com, August 10, 2009, thread #487108
[135] Temple of Mut website, August 12, 2009:
http://templeofmut.wordpress.com/

Also on August 12th, Representative Gene Green (D-TX) announced on his website that he would begin requiring attendees at his Town Hall meetings to show photo identification to prove they lived in his district. He stated the purpose of this action was due to a "coordinated effort to disrupt our town hall meetings," and that he had already experienced four meetings characterized by "shouting and interruptions". Green continued, "While I regret this restriction, it is necessary for the safety and consideration of our constituents. Those who do not reside in the 29th congressional district should contact their member of congress."

Republican members noted that Green had voted against a GOP amendment that would have required Medicaid recipients to prove citizenship with a photo ID. "It's just a tad ironic that while Congressman Green forces his own constituents to produce photo ID simply to attend a town hall meeting, he doesn't feel it necessary that people who receive government subsidies should do the same," said Brad Dayspring, spokesman for House Minority Whip Eric Cantor (R-VA). [136]

Senator Arlen Specter (D), continuing his Pennsylvania Town Hall tour, sans Secretary Sebelius, was in the town of Lebanon on Tuesday, August 11th. One of the questioners was Katy Abrams, whose bout with the Senator became a You Tube sensation. Ms. Abrams later appeared on Fox News *"Hannity's America"*, and with Lawrence O'Donnell on MSNBC's *"Hardball"*.

---

[136] The Hill "Rep. Green to Require Photo ID at Town Halls" by Mike Soraghan, August 12, 2009:
http://thehill.com/index2.php?option=com_content&task=view&id=85001&pop=1&page=0&Itemid=70

Abrams began, "I'm a Republican, and I'm a conservative," she said in a measured voice. "I don't believe this is about health care or TARP. It's about the systematic dismantling of this country." Over the approving applause she continued, "I'm 35 years old and I haven't been interested in politics until now."

She paused and stated clearly, "You've awakened a sleeping giant. We're tired of this. This is why so many here are so ticked off. I don't want us turning into Russia or a socialist country. My question for you is — what will you do to restore our country back to what our founders intended and restore the Constitution?" The crowd jumped to their feet in a standing ovation accompanied by cheers and whistles.

The Senator responded that he always upholds the Constitution, accompanied by audible groans from the audience.[137] The crowd reaction was indicative of the disconnection between the people who understand the restraints of government under the Constitution, and those politicians who trample on individual liberty while pretending to uphold it.

The next day there was another meeting in State College , Pennsylvania. Jennifer Money, a 32 year-old stay at home mom, came to the Town Hall "to voice my opposition. They should be open and honest instead of ramming it through." Another concerned citizen attending was Nick Sidorick, a 38 year-old owner of a sports bar, who commented on the effects of high taxes on the average working American, "I work 14 hours a day and I can't get ahead because of what the government takes from me."

---

[137] You Tube Video: http://www.youtube.com/watch?v=jVijmvMHsSO

On August 13th near Pittsburgh, at the Belmont Complex in East Franklin, between 1,500 and 2,000 people stood under the hot sun in a line that snaked around the parking lot. Eventually 200 were allowed into the hall. Specter's attempts to dispel the supposed "myths" about the health care bill were often met with the well-informed crowd retorting in unison, "Read the bill!"[138]

"What's the rush, sir?" asked Trish Hamel, expressing the common concern that congress was going to pass the bill despite the citizens' overwhelming objections. The crowd reacted vocally to several of the Senator's comments, and many laughed out loud when he said he would not support a bill that increased the deficit.

A USA Today/Gallup Poll released on August 12th showed that 57% of Americans believed the sentiments of the Town Hall protesters were genuine, 34% of respondents said they were more sympathetic to the protester's viewpoint, and 21% were less sympathetic.[139]

An Internet poster observed, "Yes, they have awakened a sleeping giant. What I'd give to see some patriots raise the Gadsden "Don't Tread On Me" flag above the Capitol, Iwo Jima style."[140]

On-the-ground efforts by Democrat partisans seemed designed to leave opposition lawmakers twisting in the wind of

---

[138] Pittsburgh Tribune-Review "Angry Crowd Jeers Specter, Who Says He Won't Back Higher Deficit" by Luis Fabregas, August 14, 2009: http://www.pitsburghlive.com/x/valleynewsdispatch/S_638276.html#
[139] National telephone poll of 1,000 adults conducted August 11, 2009 with a margin of sampling error of plus or minus 4%. Reported by Chron.com "Protester Warns: 'You Have Awakened a Sleeping Giant'", August 13, 2009: http://www.chron.com/disp/story.mpl/health/6570918.html
[140] Lucianne.com website, August 13, 2009.

citizen discontent. Two Republican representatives from Illinois, Mark Kirk and Judy Biggert, sent a letter to the president complaining about Democrat operatives who scheduled meetings between them and their constituents without notification, leading the constituents to arrive for non-existent meetings.

According to Kirk and Biggert's letter, the voters in their districts had apparently signed up to discuss health care reform after they received an August 9th email from BarackObama.com. "However, the names of our constituents and the times they wished to visit were never communicated to us," stated the letter. As a result, the representatives said more than 20 people showed up at district offices when they were not expected. "When they learned neither the White House, the Democrat National Committee, or Organizing for America had passed their request to our offices, they were understandably confused and upset with the BarackObama.com email they had received."[141]

Senator Barbara Boxer (D-CA) refused to have any public meetings during the summer recess, so the Southern California Tax Revolt Coalition took the Town Hall to her downtown San Diego office, holding a rally outside the building on August 14th. Between 150 and 200 people showed up with their signs and flags at high noon.

Before the rally was over, a group of seven citizens decided to go inside and visit Boxer's office to see if they could

---

[141] Fox News "Roadblocks Devised to Push Back Against Health Care Town Hall Protesters", August 13, 2009:
http://www.foxnews.com/politics/2009/08/13/supporters-obamas-health-care-plan-push-town-hall-protesters

schedule a meeting with the Senator.[142] Inside they found the office staffed by one lone intern acting as the receptionist. She suggested the group leave their names and phone numbers and someone would get back to them. A woman in the group insisted on speaking to the supervisor, and after a few minutes the intern was able to get her on the telephone.

The field representative explained that she would be unable to schedule a meeting for them with the Senator, as Boxer had not been to the San Diego office personally in over two years. The staffer did meet with the group a few days later and heard their concerns about the health care bill, took detailed notes, and promised she would pass their comments along to the Senator.[143]

It is unknown if those comments were forwarded on to the Senator in any meaningful format, or for that matter, if the Senator even bothered to look at them or consider them seriously.

On the August 16th broadcast of ABC's *"This Week"*, Senator Arlen Specter commented on the raucous Town Hall meetings he had experienced. "I think we have to bear in mind that although those people need to be heard and have a right to be heard, that they're not really representative of America, in my opinion." He continued, "We have to be careful here not to let those town meetings dominate the scene and influence what we do on health policy." He concluded, "We can't allow these meetings to dominate the political process. That would be destructive of what we need to do." [144]

---

[142] Temple of Mut website, August 14, 2009:
http://templeofmut.wordpress.com/
[143] Temple of Mut website, August 18, 2009:
http://templeofmut.wordpress.com/
[144] The Hill "Specter: Town Halls Shouldn't Dominate Process" by J. Taylor Rushing and Eric Zimmermann, August 16, 2009:

Plainly, the political class does not care to have citizens "dominating" the political process, and wish to totally ignore our Constitutional founding. The Progressive politicians were also making sure that any other obstacles to what they "need to do" were swept away. Among those obstacles were the private health insurance companies who were in opposition to the reform plan.

On August 20th, the House Energy and Commerce Committee, led by Henry Waxman (D-CA) and Bart Stupak (D-MI), sent a letter to private health insurers warning them that the Committee will be "examining executive compensation and other business practices of the health industry." The letter was sent without the knowledge of the Republican members of the Committee. The insurance companies viewed this action as a reprisal against their publicly expressed concerns.[145]

In less than a month individual targets began to receive direct and specific pressure.

Humana, one of the biggest insurance companies offering Medicare Advantage plans (covering medical services not included in Medicare), has policies with 1.5 million senior Americans. The company sent a letter to its enrollees explaining the probable impacts of the proposed health care reform on the policies they were currently offering. At the urging of Senator Max Baucus (D-MT), the Centers for Medicare and Medicaid Services (CMS) sent a letter to Humana accusing them of using "scare tactics" and ordered the

---

http://thehill.com/index2.php?optoin=com_content&task=view&id=85054&pop=1&page=0&Itemid=70
[145] Fox News "Health Insurers Fear Probe By House Dems is Reprisal for Opposing Part of Obama's Plan" by Carl Cameron, August 20, 2009.

company to halt all related outreach until an investigation had been concluded.[146]

The September 18th letter, from the federal agency that holds jurisdiction over Medicare Advantage insurance plans, stated, "CMS is concerned that, among other things, this information is misleading and confusing to beneficiaries...makes several other claims about the legislation and how it will be detrimental to enrollees, ultimately urging enrollees to contact their congressional representatives to protest the actions referenced in the letter." Oh, the horror. Encouraging people to protest their representative's actions, how dare they?

Senator Baucus, Chairman of the Senate Finance Committee, made the letter public, accompanied by this statement: "It is wholly unacceptable for insurance companies to mislead seniors regarding any subject — particularly on a subject as important to them, and to the nation, as health care reform." The statement was released the day before his committee was scheduled to begin debate on the legislation.

The full weight of the federal government was brought to bear on citizen activists and private industry alike for expressing an opinion different from the Progressive elites in power. However, despite their best efforts — or because of them, opposition to the government take-over of medical care grew with each passing day.

A coalition of fourteen organizations and websites joined the Tea Party Patriots in calling for a national "Recess Rally" against the

---

[146] Reuters "U.S. Medicare Probes Humana Over Letter to Patients", September 21, 2009: http://www.reuters.com/article/GCA-HealthcareReform/idUSTRE58K4Z220090921

health care take-over on Saturday, August 22nd.[147] The protests were planned for outside the district offices of House members and Senators.

The American Liberty Alliance set up a special website for reporting turnouts and posting pictures. By the 23rd they already had statistics from 44 rallies with a total participation of almost 14,000. The largest was a general rally in Orlando FL that turned out 3,000 patriots, with 1,000 also gathering in Miami. And, another 1,000 gathered outside Democrat Congresswoman Gabrielle Gifford's office in Tucson AZ. Most locations saw crowds numbering between 400 and 600 ralliers, and there were several sites with under one hundred.

In Miami they lined the street with their messages, "HR 3200—Kill The Bill", "Washington in the Healthcare Business? Over My Dead Body" and "Pull the Plug on Obamacare".

In Birmingham MI a man had printed out the entire text of HR 3200 and walked around carrying the 1,000 page package tied with string. Another personal message was "My Mom is NOT a 'Clunker'". [148]

The Internet site You Tube exploded with videos of citizens confronting the non-representing representatives in Town Halls across the country. Those that "went viral" hit the key issues

---

[147] The coalition included Redstate, American Liberty Alliance, Michelle Malkin, Smart Girl Politics, FreedomWorks, American Majority, Net Right Nation, The Sam Adams Alliance, Defiance Not Fear (Tea Party Express), Patriots First, Americans for Prosperity, National Tea Party Coalition, Tea Party Patriots, Let Freedom Ring, and Americans for Limited Government.
[148] Recess Rally website, August 23, 2009: http://recessrally.com/

important to freedom loving citizens opposed to the government take-over of health care, banks, energy, and car companies. Other sites also posted these videos, plus those from cameras and cell phones of participants. The videos were favorite forwards in emails. The website, Gatasi, aggregated over 20 of the most popular You Tube videos under the simple heading "Town Halls".[149]

One such video was taken at the Town Hall with Congressman Brian Baird in Clark County WA on August 18th. David Hedrick opened his comment to the Representative by identifying himself and stating that he was from Camas. "First of all I want to let everybody know that since this is the thing tonight, that I'm a Marine Corps vet." The crowd cheered and applauded, and Congressman Baird thanked him for his service. Hedrick stated, "And, like you, I did swear an oath to defend my Constitution against all enemies, foreign and domestic." Again the crowd erupted in cheers and applause.

He continued, "Now I heard you say tonight about educating our children, indoctrinating our children, whatever you want to call it." (This was a reference to a video of Obama scheduled to be shown to all school children the first week of September. The video was to be accompanied by lesson plans for teachers to guide their pupils in identifying ways they could "help" Obama further his agenda.)

Baird interrupted defensively, "No, I didn't say indoctrinating. I never said that." The crowd responded with

---

[149] Gatasi Best You Tube Videos website:
http://www.gatasi.com/tag/townhalls

188

laughter. Hedrick replied emphatically, "Stay away from my kids!" There were more cheers and applause.

Hedrick continued, "I also heard you say that you're gonna let us keep our health insurance." Then he added disdainfully, "Well, thank you!" Continuing in a forceful tone he stated, "It's not your right to decide whether or not I keep my current plan. That's my decision." Again, the audience responded with cheers and spirited applause.

Hedrick stated, "Now I've heard recently in the media you and some other people on the national political stage call us Brown Shirts because we oppose it." ("Brown Shirts" was the name given to the Hitler storm troopers that used violence to quell dissent from the German people against the Nazis.) Baird had made a comment, on August 7, 2009, in a phone interview saying, "What we're seeing right now is close to Brown Shirt tactics. I mean that very seriously."[150]

Baird, once again on the defensive, said, "No, I did not. No, I did not. What I said was", the rest of his comment was drowned out by boos and shouts from the crowd.

He weakly continued, "I, and I've apologized for it."

"Ok, well thanks," acknowledged Hedrick. "Thanks for apologizing, but I won't speak to you then, I'll speak to others. But I'll remind you, a little history lesson. The Nazis were the National Socialist Party. They were leftists. They were. They took over the finance. They took over the car industry. They took over health care in that country."

---

[150] Posted on Right Pundits.Com website, August 8, 2009:
http://www.rightpundits.com/?p=4548

Amid the enduring cheers, Hedrick continued, "If Nancy Pelosi wants to find a swastika, maybe the first place she should look is the sleeve of her own arm!" The crowd went wild.

"Now what I want to know is, you've done a lot of things that violate your constitutional oath, as you know."

Hedrick concluded, "What I want to know is, as a Marine, as a disabled veteran that served this country, I've kept my oath. Do you ever intend to keep yours?"

Baird meekly responded, "Yes, I do."[151]

The Town Halls continued on into the beginning of September, and on the 5th a small business owner took on Congresswoman Lynn Woolsey (D-CA) in Petaluma. The video was an instant Internet hit, and portions of the audio were played on talk radio shows across the nation.

The petite blond woman began simply, "My name is Catherine Bragg, and I am from Novato, California. I'm also a small business owner." She continued in a measured tone, "Right now, 90% of the businesses in the United States help support this financial system that we have in place, small business like myself." The crowd responded with supportive applause.

"Now, the problem I have is that both sides of the political aisle have tried to put reformation on health care out there for years." Bragg continued emphatically, "and nobody has done anything until today and now it's being rammed down our throats!" The audience enthusiastically cheered. She stated

---

[151] Gatasi Best You Tube Videos website:
http://www.gatasi.com/tag/townhalls

firmly, "Now, I have contacted your office in the past when I've opposed anything, " then with scorn she added, "and I get back the standard email that says, 'Thank you for your support'!"

"That's a bunch of bull," she vigorously declared. "When I speak in opposition, I expect respect! We've called your office and your staff has told us that you know best when I oppose it!" Almost entirely drowned out by the supportive boos of the crowd, Woolsey is heard to say defensively, "That's not true."

An animated Bragg went on without missing a beat, "Now, right now in California, as a small business owner, I could use tort reform!" Over the rising cheers of the crowd she emphasized, "As a small business owner, I could use competition! There are thirteen-hundred insurance companies in the United States and six of them – I can only use six in California!" The cheering became sustained and raucous.

Circling her hand in the air, she declared, "If you open it up to competition, like I experience in my business — competition makes me better!" And, while lowering her hand over her heart she affirmed, "And in the end, I do not try to overcharge anybody! I don't try to gouge anybody!" Bragg triumphantly concluded, "If you let the free market system work, everybody can have insurance!"

The crowd erupted in a standing ovation with a wave of cheering and applause that rose to the rafters. Bragg turned and after a few steps was taken up into the arms of her husband, who lifted her feet off the floor in a hug of great love and pride.[152]

---

[152] Ibid.

One of the largest Tea Parties during the August congressional recess was a massive rally in Sacramento to protest the economy killing regulations imposed on Californians in the pagan-sacred name of "the environment". The theme of the August 28th rally was the ever-growing "Eco-Tyranny" that was strangling the once great Golden State. What has happened in California must serve as a warning to our sister states.

For decades the Progressive-dominated Democrat Party has controlled the state legislature. In 2006 they passed AB 32, the "Global Warming Solutions Act", modeled on the Kyoto Protocol, to combat the false concept of man-made global warming. The California Air Resources Board (CARB) was designated the lead agency for the writing and enforcement of regulations designed to reduce the state's greenhouse gas emissions to 1990 levels by 2020, a theoretical 25% reduction of emissions from "business as usual" estimates.

The regulations will impose new restrictions on vehicle emissions, building codes, and establishes a Cap and Trade system for factories and power companies scheduled to begin in 2012. Gasoline and residential heating fuel suppliers will also be included in the Cap and Trade scheme. The state plans to regulate nearly every source of emissions to reach the draconian goals of AB 32.[153]

Since 1998 a major component of CARB's regulatory action has been the concept of "clean" vehicles, and those regulations have forced companies that rely on diesel equipment

---

[153] Climate Change Scoping Plan: A Framework for Change, December 2008, Pursuant to AB 32 The California Global Warming Solutions Act of 2006: http://www.arb.ca.gov/cc/scopingplan/document/adopted_scoping_plan.pdf

to comply or close. The author of the CARB study on diesel soot effects, Hien Tran, has acknowledged that he falsified his credentials and did not possess a doctorate from the University of California, Davis. Mr. Tran was demoted from his position, but did not lose his job. The report remained unchanged.

In July 2008, Dr. S. Stanley Young, an official of the National Institute of Statistical Sciences, pointed out in a letter to Governor Arnold Schwarzenegger that, "none of the authors (of the report) are professional statisticians".[154] Despite the problems with the study's author and statistical conclusions, CARB is now demanding that trucking companies, construction firms, timber operations, and any business using diesel engines, retrofit or replace their vehicles and equipment.

A 2009 study by economists at the California State University at Sacramento and commissioned by the California Small Business Roundtable found that the annual costs to the state government of AB 32 could total over $100 billion dollars, with consumers paying an annual cost of $3,857 per household by 2020. Another study commissioned by the Governor's Office of Small Business Advocacy estimates the direct cost of these regulations is $175 billion, or nearly twice the size of the state general fund budget. Costs to small businesses would be $134,000 per year.[155]

---

[154] *The Sacramento Bee*, "Air Board's Cover-up Casts Pall on Diesel Rules" by Dan Walters, December 2, 2009:
http://www.sacbee.com/politics/story/2363161.html
[155] *The Wall Street Journal*, "California Cap-and Trade Revolt", January 11, 2010:
http://online.wsj.com/article/SB100014240527487035809045746381533427
23572.html?mod=googlenews_wsj

AB 32 was not the worst or only issue at the heart of the Eco-Tyranny rally. The most immediate and pressing problem was the irrigation water shut-off to the farmers of California's fertile Central Valley. California leads the nation in agriculture, producing 12% of the food consumed in America, with Fresno County alone growing 40% of the world's processing tomatoes. Utilizing a radical interpretation of the Endangered Species Act, a Federal Court judge ordered the shut-off of life-sustaining water from the irrigation canals in the richest farmland of the nation, for the benefit of the Delta Smelt. The Smelt is a three-inch fish that most of the country would consider bait. As the once full canals ran dry in the summer of 2009 over 500,000 acres became fallow and turned to dust. It is estimated that the farmers and fruit growers lost $17 million and unemployment in the Central Valley rose to an unprecedented 40%.

The Community Food Bank in Fresno was serving 30,000 people a month by August 2009. The valley that fed the nation now had to have relief food brought in because of a government-made drought.

The great economic engine of California was grinding to a halt because Progressives had slowly radicalized the original and legitimate environmental movement. It is used now as a tool to clamp down on free market capitalism and ultimately replace it with a government-run economy. Productive businesses, large and small, farmers, loggers, fisherman, and truckers were being stifled by onerous regulations and court decrees handed down by the intellectual elites. California is the template for Progressive policies and the radical left intend to impose these business and job-killing regulations upon the rest of the nation under federal Cap and Trade legislation.

Responding to these dire circumstances, Mark Meckler and the Tea Party Patriots organized the August 28th rally on the steps of the California State Capitol in Sacramento. The local talk and news radio station KTKZ 1380 AM broadcasted live from the event. Although the rally was scheduled to begin at noon, by 10:00 a.m. there were already several hundred people gathering and visiting the information booths set up around the perimeter of the central lawn.

One of the booths belonged to the Howard Jarvis Taxpayers Association. Karen Klinger, a youthful real estate agent, was busy distributing literature and talking with the folks who stopped by for information. In a short-lived lull between people she emphasized, "It's about the spending!"

At another booth, Katie Kilbane, a young mother, was collecting signatures on a petition to turn on the water pumps. "Anger is growing because it's all so important. Everything that is happening today affects my generation's kids and grandkids." Kilbane continued, "We have to balance our checkbooks and when we don't have money we don't buy things. They should have to do the same." A nearby sign proclaimed, "Congress Created Dust Bowl".

A small group, from the Central Valley town of Hanford, was gathered under two professionally printed banners. The first read, "Stop Eco Tyranny—We Need Farm Water For Families + Patients + Community: H_2O = Lifeblood, Health & Jobs". The second was a take-off on a popular credit card commercial,

"80,000 Jobs—Lost, Fruit Trees—Dead, Topsoil—Eroded, 2-inch Bait Fish—Priceless". Dennise Peterson, who has been the office manager for her husband's dental practice for 25 years, organized the Hanford group. Referring to the national health care reform bill, she said, "We take personal responsibility to give health care in our community. The government will have to raise taxes to take care of this. There is no money to provide what is in this health care bill." She continued, "We now have 25% poverty in our area because of the loss of water and loss of jobs. The money is gone. The first ten pages of HR 3200 give the executive branch control over it all." She then asked, "What's this about all the czars?" and throwing up her hands declared, "I can't take it!"

Chris Smith, a female long-distance trucker in her mid 30's, was part of a group from Chico who arrived in a full bus followed by a convoy of nine cars. Commenting on the effect of the Town Halls on elected officials she said, "I don't think it matters what Pelosi says. They say one thing and do another. We are the ones to defend the Constitution, because no one else is doing it." Regarding the issues surrounding AB 32 she animatedly asked, "When have you seen farmers and truckers on the same side of an issue? More than anything else, we have to keep this movement going by making change at the local and state level."

As the crowd continued to fill the capitol lawn many carried signs displaying their own personal messages for the Speaker of the House: "Hey Pelosi—No AstroTurf Here", "Pelosi—Don't Botox My Freedom" and "If You Worked For Me, I Would Fire You". Other signs declared, "If You Have A

Job—Thank A Capitalist" and "No Freedom, No Peace, No Peas". An estimated 8,000 patriots gathered at the peak of the rally.

On 9th Street, which runs in front of the west steps, four farm tractors were displaying a large banner reading, "No Water, No Jobs = No Future". Several large groups of farm workers from the Sacramento Delta region and the Central Valley held signs proclaiming, "Farmers: Endangered Species", "Save The Farms, Let The Fish Go" and "If You Like Foreign Oil, You'll Love Foreign Food". The rally was kicked off with a convoy of seventeen farm tractors that had been driven up from the Central Valley, effectively closing 9th Street to any other vehicular traffic. The farm convoy was joined by ten dump trucks that honked their horns as they circled the Capital block throughout the four-hour rally.

A prominent figure on the stage was a large replica of the Statue of Liberty standing to the right of the speakers' podium. When the program opened with Lisa Marie Allison singing the National Anthem, the crowd robustly joined her. KTKZ talk host, Eric Hogue, performed the duties of Master of Ceremonies, and began with a call for veterans of the armed forces to come forward to the area in front of the stage. In honor of fallen comrades and heroes, a bugler played "Taps" to the hushed and reverent crowd. In the following silence Mark Meckler's children led the assembly in the Pledge of Allegiance.

The majority of the speakers were everyday working Californians including farmers, loggers, miners, manufacturers, and truckers. Walter Bransom, a fourth generation California miner from the small town of Rough and Ready, spoke on behalf of independent miners and the effect of emission controls on their equipment. Peter Allen, from the group "Water for All", spoke in Spanish (with English translation) of the plight of farm workers. He ended with a plea to the occupants of the state house to "turn the water on!" Some of the nearby signs proclaimed, "Water Not Welfare" and "Endangered Species—Small Business Owner". A man was seen wearing a t-shirt identifying himself as a member of the "Tyranny Response Team". A sign nearby asked, "Did I Fall Asleep and Wake Up in Venezuela?"

Gabriella Holt, from California Citizens for Reform, spoke on the group's initiative to return the state to a part-time legislature. Holt explained, "Businesses are leaving the state because of over regulation. The next endangered species should be the California legislature." Other speakers included Congressman Devin Nunes, State Assemblyman Dan Noe, and a representative from the Howard Jarvis Taxpayers Association.

Interspersed between the speakers, live entertainment kept the crowd fired up. A featured entertainer was Lloyd Marcus, a member of the Tea Party Express. He sang the Tea Party's favorite song, "2010" (to the tune of "New York, New York") backed by a kick-line of Tea Party gals, and "Proud To Be An American" dedicated to current and former military members. Shortly after his performance, at 2:45 p.m., the crowd bid farewell to the Tea Party Express buses as they headed for their first rally in Reno NV on their cross-country trip to the 9-12 March on Washington D.C.

————————————

As spirited skirmishes and face-to-face duels defined the national battle lines during the August congressional recess, it became ever more apparent that well over half of the population opposed the major agenda issues proposed by the Progressive Democrats. And a sizable percentage of those citizens were willing to publicly demonstrate and actively fight that agenda.

The American people were at war with their own government for the preservation of individual liberty. It was a war they were determined to fight civilly and without violence on their part, as befits the free and open society bequeathed to us by our founders.

The continued denial by elected representatives of the validity of the people's concerns angered some, aggravated most, and motivated all. When officials began to use the weight and force of government on dissenters, liberty-minded citizens realized it was going to be a long, hard fight with many battles. They remembered that the first patriots did not achieve independence in 1776 by simply signing a document. It took six years to win the Revolutionary War in 1781[156], another six before the Constitution was drafted in 1787, and four more years for full ratification by the original thirteen states in 1791.

Patriots within the Tea Party Movement became the Minute Men of the American Revolution 2.0, and along with other groups began to plan long-term strategies and prepare short-term tactics. Local Tea Party Patriot groups began organizing email and phone campaigns, and calling for rallies, sometimes on short notice, outside

---

[156] The first armed confrontation between the Rebels and the Redcoats was at Lexington and Concord on April 19, 1775.

offices and at public appearances of elected representatives. Participant numbers varied from several to several hundred, to thousands at the larger rallies. Even with only a few patriots able to respond to a "minute call", they kept themselves a constant presence in the consciousness of their non-representing representatives.

With the prevalence of the Internet videos, and postings of personal experiences at the Town Halls, patriots were inspired by the passion of their fellow same-minded citizens expressing what they themselves wanted to say. They were proud of their compatriots' spirit and the articulate presentation of their messages. Here were ordinary people really speaking truth to power, simply, honestly, directly, and forcefully. Each spoke for tens of millions of their fellow citizens.

Individuals took that inspiration and translated it into sustained action. The Tea Party rallies and Town Hall protests of the summer were the training grounds for the national rally on September 12th. The American Revolution 2.0 was heading to Washington, D.C.

Chapter Six

The March:
Can You Hear Us Now?

*"That a charter (constitution) is to be understood as
a bond of solemn obligation,
which the whole enters into,
to support the right of every separate part,
whether of religion, personal freedom, or property.
A firm bargain and a right reckoning make long friends."
- Thomas Paine, "Common Sense", 1776*

From the start of the Tea Party Movement various groups joined forces to plan and organize a national protest against the radical Progressive agenda proposed by the Democrats. The rally was to be held on September 12th at the Capitol Building in Washington D.C. The date was chosen to memorialize the united purpose of the country in the days following the terrorist attacks on September 11, 2001.

Among the groups included in the planning, organizing, and promoting of the massive march were: the 9.12 Project, Tea Party Patriots, FreedomWorks, Americans for Tax Reform, Americans for Prosperity, American Conservative Union's Club for Growth, Ayn Rand Center for Individual Rights, the Heartland Institute, National Tax Limitation Committee, National Taxpayers Union, Resistnet.com, RightMarch.com, and the Tea Party Express.

The Tea Party Express, not affiliated with Tea Party Patriots, was an outgrowth of Our Country Deserves Better PAC (Political Action Committee), which supported Republican candidates in the 2008 elections. Organizers included Mark Williams, Deborah Johns, and Lloyd Marcus. The Tea Party Express planned an initial fifteen-state, 34-city cross-country trip in 15 days. Driving two custom-painted tour buses, its final destination was the U.S. Capitol on September 12th. Besides Lloyd Marcus, other entertainers included Ron and Kay Rivoli (the Rivoli Revue), and Diane Nagy. Fox News correspondent Griff Jenkins joined the tour and provided live reporting on the events throughout the 2-week trek.

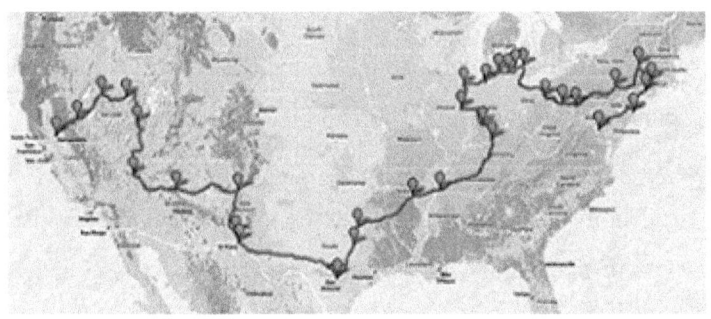

After leaving the Eco-Tyranny rally in Sacramento, their first stop in Reno/Carson City NV was an evening rally with over 500 patriots. Day 2 and 3 saw the Express rolling through the Nevada towns of Winnemucca, Elko, and Ely drawing crowds of several hundred in these small desert communities. Their last stop in Nevada was that state's largest city, Las Vegas, with mid-morning rally on Day 4, drawing a crowd of about 900 citizen activists.

Beginning their trip across Arizona, they were met by a throng of over 1,000 at the closed Honda dealership on old Route 66 in Flagstaff. The rally began with a speech by Mark Williams, national radio talk show host and vice chairman of Our Country Deserves Better. Williams called for citizens to "take our country back", as he addressed the threat of socialism and the increasing amount of taxes being imposed by congress. "Government is too big, it's too intrusive," stated Williams. "Stop raising our taxes. We all know we've got to pay taxes, right? But, for the essential services of the government, not the fantasies and the delusions of the Marxists and the Socialists who have us by the throat."

Also speaking was Arizona State Treasurer Dean Martin, addressing the problem of the government spending money it does not have and looking to the people to pay the debt. "All of you came here today to send a message," declared Martin. "We're tired of irresponsible spending. We're tired of runaway government. We are sick and tired of them treating us as an ATM."

Taking up the topic of the proposed health care bill was Tom Jenny, the Arizona director of Americans for Prosperity. "All roads lead to the government telling you that you have to get this plan. And they tell you that the plan will include this and this and at the end of the day, that means the government will decide who lives and who dies. In the case of national health care, that is literally the choice — liberty or death."

The Arizona Democrat Party vice-chairman, Matt Capably, echoed Nancy Pelosi's *USA Today* editorial by proclaiming that the Tea Party was "unpatriotic", and did not merit a counter protest from Democrats. "It's the view of the party that [the Tea Party rallies] don't really deserve a response," sniffed Capably. He continued dismissively, "I don't even know what they're complaining about. They're just posturing because they're upset that they lost the election. The issues they're raising now border on the absurd."[157]

On Day 5, September 1st, the tour crossed into New Mexico with an afternoon event in Albuquerque, and an evening rally in Las Cruces, drawing crowds into the hundreds at each location. September 2nd saw the tour begin their three-day leg through the state of Texas, with their first stop in El Paso. The following day there were rallies in San Antonio and Waco.

Meanwhile in California, on September 3rd, violence again erupted when an opponent of the health care bill had part of his finger bitten off by a member of the anti-war group Code Pink. In the city of Thousand Oaks about 100 supporters of the health care bill were having a rally sponsored by the Progressive organizations MoveOn.org and Code Pink. A group of health care protesters formed across the street. The victim, William Rice age 65, became involved in a heated discussion with members from Code Pink. After the exchange, Rice returned to his own group across the street. A Code Pink member followed Rice. He then began to verbally confront Rice and acted aggressively. Rice later told investigators that he felt threatened by the man and had

---

[157] Flagstaff AZ rally as reported by JackCentral.com news:
http://jackcentral.com/news/2009/09/tea-party-express-rallies-protestors-in-flagstaff/

punched him in the nose. During a fistfight between the two men, the tip of Rice's left pinky finger was bitten off. The suspect fled the scene, and Rice drove himself to the hospital. Another man found the bitten-off portion of the finger and brought it to Rice at the hospital.[158]

Once again, the inability of the Progressive left to effectively discuss their policies resulted in violence perpetrated upon those who disagree with their view of utopia.

Many representatives chose not to hold Town Halls throughout the congressional recess, however they were continually being challenged by their constituents to have public meetings. One such was Representative Gabrielle Giffords (D-AZ). She finally relented and between September 2nd and 3rd she was met by thousands of people at Town Hall events in Sierra Vista, Green Valley, and Tucson.

The Tucson Town Hall on September 3rd drew an estimated 3,000 to 4,000 people, quickly filling the 1,500-person capacity of the Sahuaro High School auditorium and the 1,000 seats available outside. The event was scheduled to begin at 6:00 p.m., but people began to line up for seats at 2:00 p.m.

Trent Humphries and Robert Mayer, organizers of the Tucson Tea Party, wrote on their website, "It was obvious to anyone in attendance that 2/3 to 3/4 of the people there were against the public option. In fact, when one man suggested that we throw all the bums out of Congress, nearly 90% of the people

---

[158] "Man's Finger Bitten Off in Scuffle at Health Care Rally", by KTLA News, September 3, 2009: http://www.ktla.com/news/landing/ktla-finger-bitten-rally,0,1692968

in the auditorium gave him a standing, shouting ovation that lasted nearly two minutes." Humphries and Mayer continued, "That theme replayed all night. When 'facts' were presented by Giffords or her supporters that everyone knew to be false, she was met with a loud round of boos. When she declared her support for the public option, the boos and jeers could have toppled buildings with their intensity."

Humphries and Mayer wrapped up their report, "Even with hundreds of Tea Partiers in attendance, there was no way that we could have brought such large opposition alone. From what we could tell by last night, the American people are truly waking up to what their government is doing. They are becoming motivated and involved. The tide is finally changing."[159]

On September 4th, White House Press Secretary, Robert Gibbs, appeared on CNBC's "*Squawk on the Street*" program with Washington correspondent John Harwood. Harwood asked Gibbs why the administration decided to go after Rick Santelli following his famous February 19th call for a tea party at Lake Michigan in opposition to the home modification plan.

Gibbs replied, "Truthfully, one primary reason. And that was, I thought the argument that he was making was both disingenuous and not based on the facts. It was clear that Rick was very passionate about the issue. And look, we have differing opinions from both sides of the political aisle. It was clear to me that the argument that he was making wasn't based on him having

---

[159] Trent Humphries and Robert Mayer, Tucson Tea Party website, September 4, 2009: http://www.tuconteaparty.org/?p=384

actually read our plan." (Isn't it the height of hypocrisy that the spokesperson for the Democrat regime would fault someone for not reading the legislation?)

Santelli replied to Gibbs' comments later that day on CNBC's program *"Power Lunch"*. "There's two points that I want to clarify. He once again continues, Mr. Gibbs, to say that I was disingenuous and didn't read the home modification plan. Just for the record, not that it really matters, I did. But what's even more important is the part of the conversation with John Harwood and Mr. Gibbs that was missing, and that is something magical and uniquely American happened on the 19th and 20th of February."

Santelli continued, "The American people want to be heard. And unlike many countries if you don't agree with your government, it's OK in this country, to get together, to have Tea Parties, to have bus rides of Tea Parties, and to challenge in Town Hall meetings." Santelli concluded, "I think we should all be proud that we are living in a country where we can question those we put in power because at the end of the day they work for every citizen. I think that is a great aspect that came out and I think that it needed to be said."[160]

Back on the tour, the Tea Party Express began their eighth day with their first large on-the-road rally in Dallas TX, with a Friday morning turnout of 2,500 patriotic citizens. That

---

[160] NewsBusters.org, "Still Bitter: White House Goes After Santelli Again, but Santelli Fires Back", by Jeff Poor, September 4, 2009: http://newsbusters.org/node/32534

crowd was out done by another huge rally in Little Rock held at the Arkansas State Capitol, late in the day on September 4th.

In the crowd of 3,000 were Charlie Johnson and his wife. "The buses were late because of large crowds in Dallas and at a 'whistle stop' along Interstate 30 at the Texas-Arkansas state line. They expected about 50 people, but found 2,000."

Johnson carried a sign at the rally that proclaimed sarcastically, "Bite Me AARP". The AARP (American Association for Retired Persons) prominently supported the Obama Administration and Democrat congress' proposed health care reform bill. As a result they began to hemorrhage supporters, losing a reported 60,000 memberships between April and July 2009.

Johnson said proudly, "My sign was a big hit and I was asked to pose for many photographs." He and his wife helped to send off five from their local Tea Party Patriots group who were caravanning to the nation's capitol. Johnson concluded, "I did contribute money to this effort, and I've already made a contribution to the next Tea Party Express being organized now [October-November 2009 tour]. Last year I made contributions to John McCain and the Republicans, but I don't anymore because sadly, I can't find much to support there either."[161]

Ron and Dale Broadaway were also part of the crowd that day in Little Rock. Dale relayed, "My husband and I are 72 years old and have never marched or demonstrated before, but I became so frightened for my country that I felt it was the least I could do." Dale explained, "I have two fourth great-grandfathers and one

---

[161] Charlie Johnson: Electronic mail September 21, 2009.

fifth great-grandfather who fought in the Revolutionary War, and I will not let what they did go for nothing. People are frightened by this President's policies, and they are tired of the politics practiced by both parties. We feel that they aren't listening to us and we need to take back our country." Dale elaborated on her concerns, "The government is getting too big, just the sheer amount of debt that we have incurred and they want to add more. We can't sustain the spending. Our children and grandchildren are going to have to pay for this." She concluded, "I think they believe that we will go away, but they are misjudging the anger of the people. I have never felt so enthused about politics before, and am encouraged by knowing that there are so many people who feel as I do."[162]

After the Little Rock rally, the Tea Party Express headed to Louisville, KY for a late afternoon event on Saturday, September 5th, with 2,000 more patriots.

Saturday also saw what has to be the largest Town Hall held during the summer, in West Chester Township, Ohio. Co-sponsored by the Cincinnati and Dayton Tea Parties, the rally was held on the lawn in front of the National Voice of America Museum of Broadcasting.

The crowd continued to grow throughout the afternoon, with an estimated 18,000 attending at the peak of the rally, according to Butler County Sheriff Richard K. Jones. The event drew people from all around the region to participate in the meeting featuring Republican U.S. Representatives Jean Schmidt and Michael Turner,

---

[162] Ron and Dale Broadaway: Electronic mail September 26, 2009.

Ohio gubernatorial candidate John Kasich, and House Minority Leader John Boehner in his home district.

"It was college football's opening day, and we were looking at some serious competition," stated Chris Littleton, one of the event's coordinators. "These people came out to talk about their personal liberties being taken away instead. People are engaged and the movement is going to continue to gather steam and momentum. People are saying, 'I'm going to make my voice heard.'"

After his Town Hall segment, Representative Boehner declared, "These people are saying enough is enough. They're scared to death." Boehner continued, "They're scared that the country they grew up in is not going to be the country their children and grandchildren grow up in." The personal messages from the crowd proclaimed, "No Tax Slavery", "It's Time to Drain the Swamps in DC" and "Socialism—Rich or Poor You Will Hate It".

Wendy Jenkins, a member of the Libertarian Party, stood out among the crowd with a sign that stated, "I Am Ashamed I Voted for Obama". Jenkins explained that she thought it was the right decision when she voted for Obama, but she no longer feels that way. Regarding her sign she said, "I had to be honest about it. If the government would follow the laws of the Constitution, we would be fine."

Less than a half-mile away, a group gathered to declare their support for the health care plan. They had 20 demonstrators.[163]

---

[163] Middletown Journal, "Issues, not Politics, Is Their Cup of Tea", by Dave Greber and Lauren Pack, September 5, 2009:
http://www.middletownjournal.com/news/middletown-news/issues-not-politics-is-their-cup-of-tea-283653.html

On Sunday, September 6th, the Tea Party Express rolled into Bloomington IN, and was greeted by a roaring crowd of 1,500. Dr. Theo on the blog "Dakota Voice" reported, "Throughout the event there were spontaneous eruptions of the crowd chanting 'USA! USA! USA!', "We the People!" and "God bless the USA!"[164] After Bloomington, the Tea Party Express wrapped up their Sunday with an afternoon rally in Champaign IL.

Day 11, September 7th, began with a blockbuster mid-morning event in Joliet IL. Over 6,000 people gathered together at The Commons Performing Arts Pavilion, a hillside venue that hosted one of the largest rallies of the bus tour. Despite being held only 36 miles from the Chicago Loop, the *Chicago Tribune*, who describes itself as "The Midwest's Largest Reporting Team", did not run the story. The tour rounded out the day with two more rallies in South Bend IN and Battle Creek MI.

The next day the tour continued through Michigan with stops in the cities of Jackson and Troy, with thousands in attendance. Over 5,000 patriots greeted the buses at a morning rally on September 9th in Canton OH, followed by the first Pennsylvania stops in Franklin Park (Pittsburgh) and Johnstown. The next day saw rallies in Scranton PA and Albany NY.

Thousand-plus crowds had become the norm in each city. On Friday, September 11th, getting ever closer to their final destination of Washington D.C., the tour's last day began with a morning rally in Hartford CT, followed by an afternoon event in Bridgeport CT, and a final evening rally in Toms River NJ.

---

[164] DakotaVoice.com, September 7, 2009:
http://www.dakotavoice.com/?p=24616

The cross-country bus tour of the Tea Party Express offered a venue for local folks along-the-way to share their opinions, and it raised awareness about the national 9-12 March on Washington D.C. The significant numbers attending the tour's rallies, from small towns to large cities, indicate that a high level of awareness already existed among the citizenry. The tour inspired many to caravan with the buses, or just to head directly to D.C. themselves.

In the week prior to September 12th, hundreds of thousands of patriots began to arrive in Washington D.C., filling up hotels and the spare bedrooms of family and friends, to be part of the largest gathering of concerned average citizens to ever converge on the nation's capitol. Americans came from every state in the union, including Alaska and Hawaii, all paying their own way and on their own volition. They came singly and in groups.

Several generations of families came, from children to grandparents. They came in cars, planes, trains, and in over 450 chartered buses. Travel agencies offered special transportation and hotel packages specifically for that weekend.

The Internet sites were ablaze with posters who shared their plans with fellow patriots. On September 9th, just one thread on Lucianne.com had 171 separate posts. The commitment of the people to the movement, and their excitement about the March on Washington was palpable. This is just a small sampling from the assembling "extremist angry mob":

212

- 4-5 buses from Wilmington NC. They filled up so fast it was amazing. I think this march will surprise those that say we're just a small bunch of angry right-wing crazies. This is HUGE.

- I am taking Amtrak down [from New York] and will be bright eyed and bushy tailed for the festivities. Will be wearing my LDOT (Lucianne.com) pin and an Aggie t-shirt.

- My husband and I. We briefly considered not going and then realized that if possible, it was our duty and responsibility to do what we can to try to save our beloved country. We'll be in the Florida group. See you there!

- Driving from Hampton Roads VA. Mama, my daughter, and a nice older lady from church.

- Husband and I from Newport NH. Son and his wife joining from New Jersey. Back in 1967 or 68 I was an idiot anti-Vietnam war protester at the Pentagon. I've come a long way, baby!

- From Townsend DE with two friends (who used to be longtime Dems!).

- My brother-in-law from Georgia is flying to D.C. on a full charter flight.

- Leaving tomorrow from California. Marching on Washington isn't something I ever expected to do, but I wouldn't miss this one for the world. See you there!

- Wife and I driving from Texas and picking up a senior in North Carolina.

- Myself with a girlfriend and 2 kids. Driving from Charlottesville. If ever you took time out to do something for your country, this is the time.

- My mother-in-law, newly converted from liberalism, will be there!

- Husband and I flying the red-eye from Southern California. Thrilled to meet and march with the patriots.

- To those in Washington D.C. – for every person who is attending they are representing maybe 100+ more who could not attend. PAY ATTENTION!

- I'll be there. Hosting additional protesters from out-of-town. Note: none of us are getting paid, no one recruited us.

- 9-12 group in Rochester NY – 3 buses to D.C. I'll be going to Washington and so will my brother. Why is that interesting? Because I am a lifelong Conservative Republican, and he is a lifelong Democrat. We're both upset about the way the country is heading, and our elected officials' moves towards socialism/communism. He calls our little trip "The Bi-Partisan Brothers March on Washington". We're gonna give 'em hell.

On Thursday, September 10th, the National Taxpayers Union (NTU) held the Liberty Summit, with Andrew Moylan, Director of Government Affairs, speaking to an enthusiastic group. The NTU also helped set up more than 250 meetings for constituents and their members of congress. Duane Parde, NTU

214

President, stated, "That means many members of congress heard from the people who pay their salaries in face-to-face meetings." This is just one example of how established political groups were assisting the grassroots movement to take their concerns to their elected representatives, and adding another dimension to the street protests — direct political action.

During the afternoon of Friday, September 11th, rally organizers were meeting in the Washington D.C. offices of FreedomWorks going over final preparations for the next day's march. At 3:42 p.m. they received a bomb threat over the main telephone line. A man told the female receptionist, "I put a bomb in your building, bitch". D.C. Metro Police evacuated the building. At 4:48 p.m. the organization put out a Twitter message saying that it turned out to be a false alarm. The organization was not happy about the disruption.[165] It was surprising to no one that the radical left would resort to a bomb threat in order to disrupt preparations, even on the anniversary of the worst terrorist attack on America. A serious, but juvenile, stunt that was just one more example of the violence or threat of violence used by the left in attempts to silence those who oppose them.

At the daily press briefing on Friday, White House spokesman Robert Gibbs claimed the administration was unaware of the rally. "I don't know who the group is," Gibbs told reporters with a shrug."[166]

---

[165] Gateway Pundit posting of ABC News report, September 12, 2009: http://gatewaypundit.blogspot.com

[166] Fox News "Tea Party Express Takes Washington By Storm", September 12, 2009: http://www.foxnews.com/politics/2009/09/12/tea-party-express-takes-washington-storm/?test=latestnews

In addition to the main March on Washington, 9-12 rallies were held in cities and towns across America. This list by no means includes all of the rallies held that day, but does give an indication of the breadth and depth of the dissatisfaction with the Progressive Democrat agenda.

- Amarillo TX — more than 600
- Beaver PA — 200-250
- Columbus GA — 250
- Effingham IL — more than 500
- El Cajon CA — 300-400
- Forsyth GA — 200
- Fort Walton Beach FL — 300
- Fort Worth TX — 2,000-3,000
- Geneva IL — 400
- Great Falls MT — 200
- Gulfport MS — 400-500
- Kankakee IL — 400
- Lakeland FL — 1,000 plus
- Lockport IL — 300-400
- Ocala FL — 500
- Odessa TX — 200-300
- Oklahoma City OK — 5,000 to 7,000
- Olympia WA — 350
- Providence RI — 300-400
- Quincy IL — more than 2,000
- Roswell, GA — 1,500
- Salem, OR — more than 1,000

- San Diego, CA —5 00-600
- Sault Ste. Marie MI — 100
- Springfield IL — 1,000
- Smithfield NC — 125
- Temecula CA — 600-700
- Tulsa OK — 500+
- Westwood (Los Angeles) CA — 2,000-3,000

One of the hundreds of thousands on the road to Washington was Woody White from Little Rock AR. Driving the distance by himself he said, "I was going to go, then I wasn't going to go because of a conflict. I finally decided that 9-12 was much more important than the conflict."

White described his arrival in Washington on Friday afternoon, "I finally found a hotel and began walking about the city around 3:00 p.m. Literally everywhere I went I ran into groups of Tea Party people from all over the country. Like me, many seemed to be amazed at the enormity of the crowds they were encountering." He continued, "At dinner in the hotel that night, the dining room was filled with Tea Partiers from Tennessee and West Virginia. Everyone was pumped up for the march, and even though I turned in early, I was so excited I could hardly sleep."[167]

The starting point for the March on the Capitol was at Freedom Plaza, a small park just east of the White House. Staging was scheduled to begin at 9:00 in the morning., but the park was

---

[167] Woody White: Electronic mail interview June 23, 2010.

already packed by 8:00 a.m. It did not take long for the area to be over capacity and by 10:00, an hour before the scheduled start time, the organizers were told by police officers that they would have to begin marching.

Pam Dashiell was among those who came in two buses from Asheville NC. "We traveled all day Friday, and didn't get into D.C. until nine-thirty that night. Then we were to be back on the buses by 6:30 a.m. for the ride to the Metro station, where we would board the train for the staging area."

Dashiell relayed, "Some of us made a quick detour from the Metro to a McDonald's for breakfast and while standing in line to order, a Metro Park Policeman, who was in an adjoining line, advised me that we 'would not have anyone at our rally.'" She continued, "He assured me that as a Park Policeman, he was 'in the know' about groups marching on a daily basis and that our group was nothing out of the ordinary. I was completely surprised that this policeman would say something like that to me when I was minding my own business. I just looked at him in disbelief and said, 'You are *wrong!*'"

Dashiell continued, "Our group returned to the Metro station and was energized when the train arrived loaded with Tea Partiers with signs and flags. Our group let out a roar when we saw the others already onboard. As we rounded the corner to the staging area, I was overwhelmed with emotion when I saw a large crowd already gathering with signs and flags galore." She remembered, "People continued to stream in and mingle among different state groups with so much enthusiasm. We had been advised that North Carolina was to be the fourth state proceeding in the march, so we stayed close to those carrying our state flag, but it became so crowded in the staging area that it was hard to move around."[168]

Also present in the staging area was Woody White from Little Rock. "I met people from Alaska who had driven to the event. I met a group of young people who had decided to take the train from Philadelphia that very morning because they were concerned there might not be a large crowd. Texas was represented by literally thousands of people, as was Arizona and New Mexico."[169]

For the next several hours, all seven lanes of Pennsylvania Avenue were filled with marchers making the 1.1-mile trip to the Capitol building for the massive rally. Pam Dashiell remembered, "It was thrilling to begin the march to the Capitol, and then to set out our chairs for a day of speeches for our causes. When we looked behind us, toward the staging area and the Washington Monument, the size of the crowd was unbelievably huge!"[170]

The overcast day deterred no one, and almost everyone carried either a homemade sign, an American or state flag, or of course, the ever-present "Don't Tread on Me" banner. Among the signs held by the marchers were, "Liberty: All the Stimulus We Need", "Stalin Called, He Wants His Policies Back" and "Dear God—Please Save America, Amen".

The establishment media low-balled the attendance estimates as "tens of thousands", Fox News reported

---

[168] Pam Dashiell: Electronic mail interview June 21, 2010.
[169] Woody White: Electronic mail interview June 23, 2010.
[170] Pam Dashiell: Electronic mail interview June 21, 2010.

"hundreds of thousands". However, there was an unbiased witness to the massive march towards the Capitol, a traffic camera on a rooftop at the corner of 14th Street and E Street NW. Considering that it took hours for the marchers to make their way down the 1.1-mile route, the crowd size could easily have topped one million.

14th and E St NW
Source : Westwood One Updates: 2 seconds

The area around the Capitol building was packed and the crowd stretched down the length of The Mall reflecting pool, even though folks that far away could not hear the speakers. The entire event was broadcast live on CSPAN.

One of those million marchers was Dawn Wildman, then a coordinator of the Southern California Tax Coalition, and eventually a member of the National Coordinators Team for Tea Party Patriots. "It was fun to be part of an event and not have to work it," began Wildman. "My father had joined me from North Carolina, and we marched together. I was carrying a California flag and many folks came up to me so excited and said, 'if California is here, this is huge'". After a pause she simply stated, "I was overwhelmed with the enormity of it all."[171]

Even as marchers were still making their way down Pennsylvania Avenue, the official program began at 1:00 p.m. with a video, produced by FreedomWorks, on large JumboTron screens located on either side of the stage set up at the foot of the steps of the Capitol. It was a "highlights show" of the out-of-control congressional spending that sparked the Tea Party Movement. As each congressional affront filled the screen, it was met with boos and jeers from the crowd.

Opening the program was Jenny Beth Martin, a co-founder of the Tea Party Patriots.[172] She declared, "We're not playing games...it's time to restore fiscal responsibility and the limited government our founding fathers intended. Let the free markets work without government intervention."

The assembled patriots roared their approval. She told the crowd she was "just an organizer" intent on giving the people a platform to express themselves. In a tone with a slight sarcastic edge, Martin continued, "Obviously the Tea Party was not loud enough in February, March, April, July or August." With emphasis she declared, "We're turning up the volume – can you hear us now?" The crowd took up the first round of the call, "Can you hear us now?"

Before the chant could die out, Brendan Steinhauser took the stage. Steinhauser, the Federal and State Campaign Director for FreedomWorks, remarked, "People paid for themselves to come.

---

[171] Dawn Wildman: Telephone interview on October 6, 2009.
[172] All quotations for 9-12 March on Washington speakers are from a video recording of the CSPAN broadcast.

This isn't ACORN, SEIU, or Organizing for America run out of the White House."

Steinhauser then introduced the founder and President of FreedomWorks, former Congressman Dick Armey and his wife. Armey took a swipe at Nancy Pelosi. "They said we were AstroTurf and we would go away!" He concluded with a quote from Benjamin Franklin, "Liberty was given to mankind by God, precious in its own right, and the duty of government is to protect it."

The crowd responded by chanting "Freedom Works!" while an instrumental of the song "America" played in the background. The homemade signs were as thick as a grove of redwoods: "Freedom for America", "Silence is Consent" and "Give Us Liberty, Not Tyranny!".

At the speaker's podium was James Anderer, a former owner of a Chrysler dealership in Lindenhurst NY. He lost his business in the auto company bailout.

Chrysler, in response to the government mandate to lower their operating costs, had closed thousands of dealerships across the country.

Anderer declared, "Due process has been corrupted, and it is proof of a government out of control. My business was stolen from me by direct action of Obama." He continued, "There was no congressional oversight and a complete manipulation of the bankruptcy courts. The Chrysler bankruptcy was controlled to conform to the Obama agenda. The unions survived, but dealerships were destroyed. 2,000 dealers closed and 150,000 workers lost their jobs. My dealership was seized and stolen from me without compensation."

"I'm an angry American," Anderer continued passionately. "I did not ask for this fight, but, my God, I'm going to win it!" The crowd enthusiastically applauded and cheered. He continued emphatically, "It happened to me and it will happen to you if we don't stop this insane march to socialism. Obama believes in the notion that government can control every aspect of an individual's life and government is the answer." He continued, "Obama thinks he has a mandate to change America. He wants it completed before the people realize what he has done. I say he's wrong." The crowd roared their agreement with these sentiments.

"We the people are in revolt against his socialist policies," Anderer declared, and began to tick off a list of presidential and congressional offences, "Because of the unconstitutional appointment of czars, because the way congress spends taxpayer dollars, because taxes are so high they are destroying our way of life, because officials don't represent us. We have let this country be taken over by people who don't believe in our values of individual liberty and personal responsibility." Anderer concluded, "The only way to get our country back is to vote them out!" The crowd responded for several minutes with a lusty chant of "Vote them out!"

Signs of the times included "Between Barack And A Hard Place", "My Wallet Is Not Shovel Ready" and "Joe Wilson For Truth Czar". The last was in reference to Representative Joe Wilson (R-SC) who spontaneously called out "Liar" during Obama's health care speech on September 9th before a special joint session of congress. The call-out was made after Obama claimed that illegal immigrants would not be included in the administration's plan.

Other signs supporting the congressman proclaimed, "Joe Wilson—Truth to Power" and "Joe Wilson Is The Hero We've Been Waiting For".

Robert Levy, Chairman of the Cato Institute, and Andrew Moylan from the National Taxpayers Union warned the crowd about the power of the federal government exerted through over 330 agencies and the inevitable rise in taxes to pay for it.

Jenny Beth Martin gave the crowd a quick update on their size and its effects, "The expressway is blocked, roads are closed, and people are still coming." She called out, "Congress, President Obama: Can you hear us now?" Once again, the refrain rang out from the gathering.

Among hundreds of American flags and Gadsden banners whipping in the breeze, the signs proclaimed the protesters' sentiments, "I Don't Belong To The Party Of No—I'm With The Party of HELL NO!", "Give Us Back Our Country or Get Ready To Be Replaced" and "Socialism Sucks—Always Has, Always Will".

Next to take the podium was Kellen Guida, the twenty-something organizer for the New York City Tea Party, who relayed the efforts of his group in going to city meetings, and out to the clubs to combat the leftist influence on the popular culture. Guida explained, "We're taking on the pop culture. We have our own counter-culture now!"

Among the entertainers between the speakers was Hi Caliber, a black conservative hip-hop rapper. The appearances of these two decidedly "hip" young men gave a stunning repudiation to the claim the Tea Party movement was racist and its ranks filled only with "old white people".

Senator Jim DeMint (R-SC) was next to take the stage. He quipped, "For the first time in a long time I'm the most popular guy in town!" He then joked, "The New York Times has reported that 500 people showed up here today." The crowd responded with a mixture of boos and derisive laughter. DeMint reminded the crowd, "The President said if we disagree with him he will call us out." He continued, "We're out. Obama welcome to Waterloo! It is a battle between big government collectivism and liberty,"

DeMint asked the crowd. "Do we keep our individualism or fall for a false hope and empty promises of government socialism and debt? I am here to stand with you and join my voice with yours. It's time for congress to stop lecturing and listen. Americans are informed and outraged, yet congress and the president don't get it. They continue with new programs and spending."

The senator concluded, "In this battle for freedom, we will win!" Among the cheering crowds was the sign, "Go Green — Recycle Congress". Other signs expressing the people's personal messages for congress included "You Work For Us" and "In God We Trust, Not Government".

Representing the average American worker was Greg Harold, a coal miner from Ohio, a citizen and veteran. He was joined on stage with a dozen other miners, holding a banner proclaiming, "Coal Miners Love America!"

Harold stated, "Every day I work for energy for everyone. The Cap and Trade bill will tax everyone, and just as Obama said, 'electricity rates will necessarily skyrocket'. The rates will cripple manufacturing. Take coal away and manufacturing jobs will go to China." Addressing the inhabitants of the Capitol Building behind him he said, "We know how you voted and we will fire you!" A sign in the crowd demanded, "Drill Here, Drill Now".

Next to take the stage was Betsy McCaughey, the patient's advocate who has been fighting the government take-over of health care since the 1990's. She brought with her the massive text of HR 3200, and the thud as it hit the podium resounded over the crowd. McCaughey stated emphatically, "There is no need to dismantle the best medical system in the world." Participant signs delivered their own personal messages: "Pull the Plug on Congress, Not Seniors", "Stop The National Socialists" and "Our Republic Is In Big Trouble".

Mason Weaver, San Diego radio host and author, approached the podium. He began by telling the crowd that he was there so they could "hear a black person talking without a teleprompter". The crowd greeted him with cheers, applause and laughter. Weaver proclaimed, "No more hyphenations, we're all Americans! If we have freedom, we don't need 'hope'". A sign in the crowd said simply, "MLK Had A Dream: What We Have Is A Nightmare".

He directed his next remarks to Obama, "We don't need you to apologize for us. We are proud of our country and culture. We are proud to be Americans." He reminded the crowd, "We win when we show up—November 2010!"

Joanne Filiatreau, one of the organizers of the Arkansas Tea Party, was a volunteer working the stage at the D.C. rally. Her father was buried at Arlington National Cemetery in January 2007. "Dad is no longer around to fight my battles for me and my children. Now it is my turn to step up to the fight, and fight it to *win*." Filiatreau continued, "The fact that our President apologized to the nations that my father fought to save, goes all through my veins. For the first time in my life, nothing makes sense. We elect senators and congressmen to go to Washington to protect our state. What I see is they are not even writing the bills that they don't read, that they vote on in the House of Representatives. We intend to 'flip the house' and take back an additional 1/3 of the Senate seats."[173] A sign in the crowd extolled, "Tea Party Patriots Fight On".

Next at the microphone was Representative Mike Pence (R-IN). He declared that the crowd was "the largest gathering of conservatives in American history". He continued, "After fighting out-of-control spending for nine years, you look like the cavalry to me!" The crowd responded with supportive cheers. Pence exclaimed, "This is a great re-awakening! We do not consent to government-run insurance and the government take-over of health care in this nation. We don't want another speech (from the president), but health care based on freedom. Every congressman should be required to read every bill and the Constitution." He concluded, "It's about who we are as a nation." One large sign

---

[173] Joanne Filiatreau: Electronic mail interview September 26, 2009.

among the crowd explained, "We Are Not 'AstroTurf', We Are Not 'A Mob', We Are Not 'Nazis', WE ARE FED UP".

Among the speakers were John Tate, President of the Campaign for Liberty, and Doc Thompson, a radio host from Richmond VA. Thompson repeated the oath of our founders, "I pledge to you, the same as the signers of the Declaration of Independence, my life, my fortune, and my sacred honor." The crowd roared its approval. He then exhorted, "Are you ready to pledge that to me? To the person next to you, and to America?"

George Benham was one of the marchers from the Benton, Arkansas group. "Several senators and congressmen should be worried about re-election." And then he added dryly, "The size of the crowd will be grossly played down in order to minimize the impact it will play on our elected officials". But, he was worried, "I fear for our country. Have we waited too late to be awakened? Is it too late to turn our country around? *I pray not!*"[174]

FreedomWorks then presented a video of the American people speaking up at the various Town Hall meetings held throughout the summer, entitled "Voices From the Grassroots".

Following the video was Amy Kremer, then a national coordinator of the Tea Party Patriots. (Kremer stepped down as a national coordinator in October 2009, and joined the efforts of the Tea Party Express.) She introduced herself as "a regular mom" from Atlanta GA, and stated, "In over 50 cities, over 30,000 Americans came out in the street on February 27th, and in 850 cities over 1.2 million showed up on April 15th." She

---

[174] George Benham: Electronic mail interview September 26, 2009.

triumphantly concluded, "Today, this is the biggest Tea Party of all!" The multitude let itself be heard in all its strength.

Other speakers included Debra Johns, from the Tea Party Express, Representative Marsha Blackburn (R-TN), Yaron Brook from the Ayn Rand Institute, and Andrew Langer from the Institute for Liberty. They continued with the theme of government over-spending, over-regulating, and over-taxing. Langer bragged, "They're scared that you know more about the legislation than they do!", and he urged the crowd to, "Cap their terms and trade them in!"

Stepping up next to entertain the crowd was Lloyd Marcus from the Tea Party Express. Before beginning his signature song "2010", he declared, "I am not an African-American. I am Lloyd Marcus, American."

As the singing and applause faded away, a special American hero stepped onto the stage, Vincent Forras. Forras is a New York City Fireman who responded to the 9-11 attacks on the World Trade Center. He remembered, "On 9-12 we had hope that America would stand together as a nation." A protester's sign promised, "We Will Take Back Our Country".

Out in the crowd was Mark Fitzpatrick, a member of the Little Rock Tea Party. Fitzpatrick explained his involvement in the movement, "The Tea Party gave me a way to express my anger and disgust over the corrupt election process and the continued corruption in Washington." He explained, "I see 'big government' as a threat to the way that we live. All I can say is that we need to educate people on how we got to be a great nation, or we are headed into a deceptive Socialist view and a totally bankrupt country."

Fitzpatrick continued, "This is the result of a biased 'main stream media' who support Obama and his radical Socialist policies. We are not able to hear the truth on ABC, CBS, NBC, CNN and others, like newspapers, so we have turned to the Internet for the real news." He concluded, "I openly speak out against these policies everywhere I go and I am getting involved in local politics, and trying to educate people to the spending that is going on in city, county and the state. I can see *no* other way to stop this communist take-over!"[175]

Other speakers included Georgia State Representative, Tom Graves (GA-12), and Mario Lopez, founder and president of the National Hispanic Leadership Fund. Lopez, the son of legal immigrants, remarked that Obama, Pelosi and Reid wanted to make the IRS Form 1040 real simple. He asked, "How much do you make?" Paused, and retorted, "Send it in!" A sign in the crowd simply stated, "Change Is Coming 2010".

Next to take the speakers' microphone was Kelly Hoag, a pretty and confident young woman. Hoag is a former U.S. Marine Captain who enlisted after the 9-11 attacks, and is a two-tour veteran of the Iraq War. She stated, "United we stand is not just a bumper sticker. We pledge our lives and our sacred honor." She concluded with a heartfelt, "God bless America!" A woman held a poignant sign that simply stated, "This Is Not The America My Dad Died For". Her sign included a photograph of her father, a service member from the Viet Nam era.

---

[175] Mark Fitzpatrick: Electronic mail interview September 26, 2009.

Hector Barreto, President of the Latino Coalition, was the Bush-appointed Administrator of the Small Business Administration from 2001-06. Barreto declared, "We don't need another trillion dollars in debt. We need common sense solutions. We need to help small business, but if you're selling more bureaucracy and less competition, we're not buying!"

Woody White from Little Rock had found himself a place on the lawn immediately in front of the Capital Building. "I visited with several of the Capitol Police who were astounded by the crowd. Several said they had never seen a crowd this big including the inauguration. They also said they had never seen a crowd that was so exuberant and yet so mindful of keeping the area clean." White recalled, "The composition of the crowd spanned several generations, all races and yet everyone was of a single purpose. They came to Washington with several agendas, but all were against government out-of-control spending and the health care reform bill."

White believes the explosion of the Tea Party Movement is due to "the growing lack-of-trust in government at all levels, but in particular the federal level." He explained, "I've never been politically active until this year, but I'm concerned about the loss of individual rights and irreversible spending programs."[176]

Several of the grassroots Internet groups that helped to organize and publicize the march were represented by such speakers as Darla Dawald from Grass Fire Resistance and William Greene from Right March Blog.

---

[176] Woody White: Electronic mail September 26, 2009 and June 23, 2010.

Greene exclaimed, "The Tenth Amendment reserves rights to the people. What the representatives are trying to do is not constitutional. They lie!" Signs in the crowd echoed those sentiments, "Liar, Liar, Liar—Wake Up America" and "Obama Lies With or Without Teleprompter".

The last speaker was Julian Kulski, a legal immigrant from Poland, an architect, WWII POW, and author of *"Legacy of the White Eagle"*. Kulski spoke with a Polish accent worn smooth by many years in America, "Thank you for pledging to defend the U.S.A." He continued passionately, "No human progress is possible under tyranny. Democratic ideals will not be realized if you are not willing to lay down your lives. There is lots to be grateful and thankful for in our great land. Continue fighting for our cherished freedom." He complimented the crowd for showing what people can do when their country needs them. Kulski concluded, "I urge you to visit Arlington Cemetery and remember who laid down their life for you. Keep the flame of America burning". The crowd responded with a hearty chant of "Freedom!"

Wrapping things up Brendan Steinhauser called on the assembled patriots to, "Flip this house!" and exhorted the crowd in one last round of chants. "Congress — Can you hear us now? President Obama — Can you hear us now?"

The afternoon of speeches ended with the crowd joining in a passionate rendition of the popular standard "God Bless America". Recorded patriotic music played low in the background as the crowd slowly began to break up. It was as if, even after the long program, no one wanted to leave.

Some Washington officials did understand the importance of the march and its potential impacts on the political landscape and history of America. The Smithsonian Institute contacted the March on Washington organizers and asked for articles from the rally. Among the artifacts donated to the nation's attic were Jenny Beth Martin's notes from that day and a t-shirt designed by Sarah Bond, of the Southern California Tax Revolt Coalition. Dawn Wildman commented, "So many things happened on the trip, just incredible gifts."[177]

Pam Dashiell, from North Carolina, summed up her experience, "At the end of the day, as we returned to the Metro station, we were able to see the crowd had been even bigger than we could envision from our position at the Capitol. I had wished to see the Metro Park Policeman from earlier on my way out to the area, but I did not run into him. Others from our group later reported to me that they had seen him at four-thirty still directing traffic due to our rally!" Dashiell concluded, "As we rode the Metro Transit back to our buses, we met and chatted with others who had driven from New York, Maryland and Connecticut to attend the rally. They, too, were pleased with our huge turn out of people who were orderly, non-confrontational, and who left the grounds of the Capitol as clean as it had been before our arrival."[178]

Tea Party people are particularly proud that their rally sites are left clear of trash. They see it as a real-world example of the principle of personal responsibility. They know that public land is *their* land and they show their stewardship by their actions.

---

[177] Dawn Wildman: Telephone interview on October 6, 2009. Ms. Wildman joined the Tea Party Patriots national coordinators team in October 2009.
[178] Pam Dashiell: Electronic mail interview June 21, 2010.

The Tea Party people left their rally site cleaner than they found it.

Not so after Obama's inauguration on January 20, 2008.[179]

---

[179] Photographs displayed on blog site "Sweetness and Light": http://sweetness-light.com/archive/120-versus-912-compare-contrast

Quite a difference from site conditions after Progressive – type gatherings, perfectly exemplified by the amount of trash in evidence following Obama's inauguration. The great irony behind the public misperception that the left *cares* more about the environment than the *exploiters and polluters* that populate the right wing mob, is that the real-world experience is the complete opposite.

Woody White was driving alone back home to Little Rock. "Along the way there was a constant honking of horns between others who had obviously attended the rally. Cars were decorated, buses were decorated, and American flags and 'Don't Tread On Me' flags flew from many of the passing cars." He continued, "I listened to numerous talk radio shows and news reports about the rally. I even called into a national show. There were people calling constantly from the road as they were driving home. Some people actually cried trying to describe the feelings they had experienced while in D.C." He concluded, "The Tea Party has had unimaginable success."[180]

In an article posted on September 16th at the Town Hall website, Brent Bozell penned a scathing piece about the biased reporting from the establishment media. Bozell wrote, "But all the media bias against this rally clearly illustrates one nagging truth for media liberals: They really don't think conservatives should be allowed to protest. It's somehow like a copyright violation."

---

[180] Woody White: Electronic mail interview June 23, 2010.

Bozell continued, "On Monday night's '*Countdown*', MSNBC's David Shuster found the protest united 'in apparent hatred of the current president, Barack Obama.' It was undemocratic, a sign of people not accepting election results, and Shuster even suggested Senator Jim DeMint's speech at the rally signaled he favored a 'military coup'. The unglued anchorman also dismissed the crowd as 'white, whiter and whitest', all attending an 'intolerance festival.'"

Recounting the coverage on one of the big three networks, Bozell wrote, "Over on ABC, anchorman Bill Weir, could find only a mob 'descending' on Washington like the flying monkeys of the Wicked Witch of the West: 'This morning: Outrage. Protesters descend on Washington to rally against the president's health care plan. As civility gives way to shouting, what's fueling all this anger?'"

Bozell concluded, "But the major media came to the rally not to develop a broad sense of the crowd's common complaint, but to isolate and humiliate conservatives by finding the lunatic fringes. The media's coverage is obviously biased, but it should cause conservatives to take heart. The tide is turning. The tea parties are scaring liberals."[181]

The 9-12 March on Washington was the physical manifestation of the people's anger and disgust towards the ruling elite. Here was the culmination of seven months of grassroots

----

[181] Town Hall, September 16, 2009 "Our 'Intolerance Festival'" by Brent Bozell: http://townhall.com/

political activism and the national debut of the formerly-silent majority.

Never before had a march on Washington been peopled by such a wide swath of the American citizenry. Prior large marches of the modern era had been for distinct and narrowly defined causes: the "Bonus March" of WWI veterans, the anti-war protests of the 1960's consisting mainly of draft-age college students, and the annual March for Life protesting the Supreme Court's Roe v. Wade decision that legalized abortion. (The March for Life has been held annually on January 22nd since the infamous decision was handed down on that date in 1973— another conservative action that is totally ignored by the establishment media. Over the last several years, the March for Life has averaged over 250,000 participants braving the often cold wintry weather.)

The difference with the 9-12 March was the wide representation, including men and women, of a variety of political party identifications, age groups, economic levels, and all races. (The demographic percentage of the various participant ranks are consistent with the general population.) While previous marches and protests were focused on a specific government policy, the 9-12 March was about the very apparatus and organization of government. Citizens were alarmed about the clear and present danger facing our most basic liberties, by a government structure that no longer represented the values of the people. The choice was as stark as it was urgent: Return to the limited government as designed in the Constitution, or abandon being a free people and become enslaved by an all-controlling oligarchy.

Americans everywhere, of all stripes and kinds, made their choice, and that choice was for the Constitution and the restoration of the limited government designed by our founders. This is the bedrock conviction held in common by every citizen who has gone to a Tea Party. As more Americans began to realize the extent of the radical Progressive agenda and its existential threat to the Republic, they made a personal choice to stand for freedom. They made their signs on the kitchen table, hopped in the car, and headed for D.C. Once there, they found themselves one million-plus strong.

If the so-called representatives had forgotten the Constitution, it was now standing before them, truly living in the presence of one million American hearts, minds and souls. It continues to live in each citizen who gathers with others in a local park, stands in front of their county courthouse, in front of their statehouse, or even in front of the U.S. Capitol Building.

"Can you hear us now?"

Conclusion

These are the times that try men's souls.
The summer soldier and the sunshine patriot will, in this crisis,
shrink from the service of his country;
but he that stands it now deserves the love and thanks
of man and woman.
Tyranny, like hell, is not easily conquered;
yet we have this consolation with us —
that the harder the conflict,
the more glorious the triumph."
- Thomas Paine, "The Crisis Papers", 1776

The Tea Party Movement is being driven by tens of millions of average citizens who have never before been active in the political arena. After decades of sitting by and watching the political class usurp the rights of the individual and the government spend public monies beyond all reason, a significant majority of Americans are fed up.

They've had enough of arrogant politicians passing laws and regulations that reach into every aspect of personal life, from low-flow toilets to mercury-filled light bulbs. They've had enough of "safety-net" social programs that expand every year to make more people dependent upon government largesse. They've had enough of cronyism that bails out banks, automakers, insurance companies, and sub-prime home mortgage lenders. They've had enough of a two-tiered justice system, one for the well connected and one for the average Joe.

By early 2009, the tipping point had been met and the vast silent majority found their voices. When they first began to make their signs and head out into the streets, they were ignored by their elected officials, or swatted away like annoying pests. The shills in the establishment media pretended they did not exist. When their growing numbers could no longer be denied, Tea Party participants were derided, denigrated, and dismissed as right-wing radicals, racists, and artificial paid-for "Astroturf" demonstrators. Yet the Tea Party people defy and repudiate this stereotyping.

The citizens participating in the Tea Party rallies are of all races, all age groups, and all political parties. They are college students and young professionals starting their careers and families. They are middle-aged folks and seniors. They are blue-collar workers and stay-at-home moms. They are veterans of our armed forces, lawyers, doctors, and nurses. They are teachers, truck drivers, and miners. They are small business owners and farm workers. All are rejecting the divisive tactics of the Progressive left, and are defining themselves today as simply, Americans.

Spearheading this movement is the Tea Party Patriots, comprising over two thousand registered groups in every state, with an aggregate total membership exceeding fifteen million (as of June 2010). The shaft of the spear is composed of FreedomWorks, Americans for Prosperity, and other established conservative action groups.

The support for the Tea Party Movement crosses all demographic lines because uncontrolled spending and ever-higher taxes threaten the security of everyone. Every age group foresees a bleak future for their children and grandchildren. Frank Luntz in his book, *"What Americans Really Want...Really,"* reports that 53% of Americans believe that when their children are their age today, they will be worse off, while only 33% think their children will be better off. This is unprecedented in America, where historically each generation has believed their children will be better off than themselves.

These Americans, whether yet part of the Tea Party Movement or not, are fed up with out-of-control government spending and tax schemes. As more members of the silent majority became aware of the impending complete Progressive/Socialist take-over of the government, they asked how the country came to be in such a dire situation.

To answer that question they started by studying the intent of our original founders. What they learned was startling. They realized that the history and values of our founding had been perverted to fit the radical left viewpoint that America was fundamentally flawed, that the capitalist free market economic system was morally evil, and that individuals could not be trusted to make their own decisions. Seen in the light of this information, the Progressive proposals were finally understood as the anti-American schemes they truly are at heart.

This awakening is displayed in the presence of every citizen at a Tea Party, and the unprecedented number of participants gives witness to the significant impact it will have on the American political landscape. One of those impacts will be the recovery of the authentic history of our country. Over the last century generations of Americans have been taught less and less about their civic duties. They learned little about our nation's great history or were taught, erroneously, that our founding fathers were not religious people, that all were hypocritical racist slaveholders, and that the Constitution was an outdated document no longer relevant in the modern world. History books were slowly rewritten over the decades, propagandizing for the freedom-stealing policies of Progressivism, in order to diminish knowledge and understanding of our unique American heritage—a heritage based on the inviolable ideals of individual liberty and personal responsibility.

The heritage of Judeo-Christian morals, the foundation of our limited government, was stripped from our schools and our public square under the constitutionally erroneous concept known as "the separation of church and state", a phrase that is nowhere to be found in the Constitution. This concept sprang from a deliberate misinterpretation, by the U.S. Supreme Court, of the First Amendment's protection of the "freedom of religion" to mean "freedom from religion".

Our founders never intended for religious or moral sentiments to be banished from the public square. Indeed, they stressed that only a moral people could maintain the liberty and freedom enshrined in the Constitution. When activist judges with Progressive ideologies removed prayer from our schools and God from public acknowledgement, they cheated the people out of their Creator-given rights to know and be guided by the values that had built our country and made it strong. Progressives deliberately filled our society with misinformation that crippled the polity mentally and spiritually.

For decades popular opinion polls showed that the majority of Americans felt that the country "was going in the wrong direction". Voters see-sawed between the Democrat and Republican parties, yet the slow march towards a totalitarian government continued, until the 2008 elections swept the radical left-wing of the Democrat Party into power.

When the Progressives gained power over all three branches of government, they abandoned their strategy of slow incremental changes, and dropped their pretence of appearing to follow Constitutional procedures. The Progressives seized their opportunity to steal the last vestiges of freedom from the American people.

Yet, in their haste the thieves made noise and the homeowner awakened. The blatant refusal of professional politicians to consider the will of the people has become the foundational issue of our time. Decades of incremental implementation of the Progressive agenda has eroded personal liberty, decayed government restraints, and corroded the balance of power. In their "let no crisis go to waste" mentality they hastily began to barrage Americans with laws that were the antithesis of freedom, and anathemas to liberty loving people everywhere.

However, the broader American experience is one of a people still rooted in the freedoms and liberties guaranteed under our Constitution. It is part of the American DNA. In the fight to conserve the Constitution, the Tea Party Movement is a vital, visible, and vocal component of that struggle.

Other facets of this reawakened citizenry are:

- Established conservative citizen-action organizations who have seen their membership rolls explode.

- Local and state elected officials who are committed to restoring limited government.

- Historians, authors, and media personalities dedicated to turning the tide against the wave of Progressive propaganda permeating our culture through our schools and the entertainment media of television, music, and films.

The fault has been in the American people for not paying attention. Our founders warned us that eternal vigilance was the price of liberty. We, as a people, did not live up to our end of the bargain. We trusted too much in the career politicians, and enabled them by not fighting the lies perpetrated by the Progressive feel-good ideology. And, now we have a country where our politicians have finally bankrupted the public treasury, trampled on the public trust, and put our Republic at risk.

The fight to restore common sense in our government is far from over. Every day the American people face a new affront to their liberties by a congress and executive branch that is more interested in power than in the people. Patriots everywhere are joining together to re-establish the Constitution as the governing document of our great land. Because if, indeed, it is a "living document" as proclaimed by Progressives, then we are no longer a nation of laws, but of the whims of man.

But, all that stops *now*. The Tea Party patriots will rescue the Constitution by electing responsible, common sense, fellow citizens to all levels of government. They will reclaim their history and celebrate the remarkable achievements of our founding fathers and mothers. They will fight the forces that seek to transform our unique Constitutional Republic into a cynical and uninspired despotism.

With one voice, the Tea Party Patriots give fair warning to their enemies both foreign and domestic: "Don't tread on me."

Yours in the Resistance,

Robin Rohr
July 4, 2010

Appendix

The Patriots' Personal Messages

Live Tea or Die

Stimulus Slave

I Am A Citizen—Not Your Subject

Share The Work And Let The Wealth Redistribute Itself

SIZE DOES MATTER—Give Me Smaller Government, Smaller Taxes, ~~Smaller~~ NO DEFICITS

SILENT NO MORE

Stop Spending My Grandkids Future

Let Us Keep Our Money

Tea Party Today, Tar and Feathers Tomorrow

Non-Partisan!! Bush—Too Much $pending,
   Obama—<u>WORSE</u> Than Bush

Obama & Congress <u>NOT</u> LISTENING—Stop $pending

Capitalism, Not Socialism and Wealth Distribution

I'll Die On My Feet, Not Live On My Knees

Public Silence Equals Public Consent

The 10th Amendment *** READ IT! HEED IT!

Queen Pelosi Says "Let Them Eat Pork"

ObamaNomics: Chains We Can Believe In

Oink If I'm Paying Your Bills

The Answer to 1984 is 1776

Silence Is Consent

PORK: The Other Green Meat

Legalize the Constitution

I Am 'We The People'

Too Much Government—Too Little Freedom

The Solution to 2009 is 1776

Work Harder, Millions on Welfare Are Counting on You

<u>God</u> Gave <u>Me</u> the Ability To Produce Wealth!! Deuteronomy 8:18, <u>Stealing</u> <u>Is</u> <u>A</u> <u>Crime</u>!!

With Any Form of Collectivism: Only the Losers Win

Right Wing <u>MAIN</u>streamist

Change is All I Have Left

John Galt Lives

Today We Are Not Democrats or Republicans—
    We're Freedom Fighters

Fed Up With The Fed and Tea'd Off

Apathy Ends Today

I Want My Country Back—And My Money

My Wallet, My Choice

Big Government is the Problem, Not the Solution

Read *Atlas Shrugged*: Now in the Non-Fiction Section

Blue Dogs—Stop Sniffin and Start Barkin for Our <u>Liberties</u>

Will Work to Keep <u>Own</u> Money

The Worst Threat To Our Freedom?—GOVERNMENT

Twinkle, Twinkle Little Czar   (with the letters made of glitter)

Silence Is Compliance

Annoy A Liberal—Use Facts & Logic

Big Govt—Stay Out of My Life

Displaying a picture of President Obama dressed as a surgeon
    saying "I'm Not A Doctor But I Play One On T.V.

DC Politicians—Kiss My Grits

Commander in Thief

Wake Up America

Stop Big Government

Less Government + Less Taxes = Liberty

End the Federal Reserve

Stop Tax & Trade

The Real Terrorists Are Congress & The Senate—
 Throw the Bums Out

Throw The Tax Spenders Out

Capitalism Is The Answer, Not Socialism

Dependency Is Slavery

Got Common Sense?

Don't Tax Me Bro!

Fake This

Repeal What You Have Not Read

Worried Democrat

Wake Up America Now or It Will Be Too Late

Official American Grassroots

No More Czars

Socialism Is Not Freedom

It's The Constitution, Stupid

Your Wallet Is The Only Place Congress Wants To Drill

Homeland Security—Here I am

We'll Keep Our Freedom And You Keep the Change

The Constitution is One Thing They Don't Read